# BODY & SOUL

## *Walking with God to Total Health*

# Further Endorsements for

# BODY & SOUL
*Walking with God to Total Health*

*Jim Maxwell has written a very comprehensive book on walking. Many of the principles in this book correspond with the concepts of the First Place program. I can heartily recommend this book to anyone interested in beginning a walking program.*

**Carole Lewis**
First Place National Director

---

*Jim Maxwell has developed a program that overcomes the excuse of "I don't have time to have a quiet time or exercise" by giving us a way to add hours to our day by combining exercise, prayer, praise, and Scripture memorization into one combined period. "For physical training is of some value, but godliness has value for all things, holding promise for both the present life and the life to come" (1 Tim. 4:8). What a great way to train the physical body while developing and growing in our relationship with Jesus Christ.*

**James B. Angel, PhD**
Chair, Exercise Science & Sports Medicine Department
Samford University

---

*Jim Maxwell has done an outstanding job in describing the relationship between your Christian and physical walk with God. Millions of Americans need to take to heart Mr. Maxwell's message.*

**David Horton, PhD**
Chair, Department of Sports Sciences
Liberty University

# BODY & SOUL

## Walking with God
## to Total Health

_____

# JIM MAXWELL

## New Hope® Publishers

Birmingham, Alabama

New Hope® Publishers

P.O. Box 12065
Birmingham, AL 35202-2065
www.newhopepubl.com

Library of Congress Cataloging-in-Publication Data

Maxwell, Jim, 1944-
Body and soul : walking with God to total health / by Jim Maxwell.
p. cm.
ISBN 1-56309-453-3 (pbk.)
1. Walking—Health aspects. 2. Walking—Religious
aspects—Christianity. 3. Christian life. I. Title.
RA781.65 .M395 2000
613.7'176—dc21
00-010174

Cover design by Rachael Crutchfield

ISBN: 1-56309-453-3
N004108 • 0900 • 7.5M1

*For Carolyn*

# Table of Contents

Preface . . . . . . . . . . . . . . . . . . . . . . . . . . . . . . . . *xi*

Chapter 1
*Walking with God* . . . . . . . . . . . . . . . . . . . . *1*

Chapter 2
*Spiritual Fitness* . . . . . . . . . . . . . . . . . . . . *11*

Chapter 3
*Spiritual Exercise* . . . . . . . . . . . . . . . . . . . *25*

Chapter 4
*Walking Alone with God* . . . . . . . . . . . . *37*

Chapter 5
*Sharing Your Walk* . . . . . . . . . . . . . . . . . . *47*

Chapter 6
*Walking for Health and Weight* . . . . . . *61*

Chapter 7
*When and Where to Walk* . . . . . . . . . . . *77*

Chapter 8
*Preparing to Walk* . . . . . . . . . . . . . . . . . . . *87*

Chapter 9
*Learning to Walk* . . . . . . . . . . . . . . . . . . . *101*

Chapter 10
*Your Personal Walking Program* . . . . *111*

Chapter 11
*Your Daily Walks* . . . . . . . . . . . . . . . . . . . *127*

Chapter 12
*Stepping Off* . . . . . . . . . . . . . . . . . . . . . . . . *141*

*Samples for Copying* . . . . . . . . . . . . . . . . . *159*

# Preface

God did not construct me to be an athlete. I was the neighborhood fat kid—the one always chosen last for sandlot baseball teams. My one serious attempt at sports was a year of high school football, and that season was our school's worst in three decades! I still refuse to accept total blame for the team's shortcomings; but the experience fit my track record for physical ineptitude.

If you question why I should write a fitness book, remember this: Fitness and good health are not just for the strong and agile. Taking care of ourselves—body and soul—is simply good stewardship of God's gifts to all who live and breathe. Anyone—not just those blessed with natural athletic ability—can enjoy fuller, richer, more meaningful living through improved fitness.

Fortunately the most effective way for most people to build physical fitness is through something that most of us already do every day: *walking*. Anyone—old or young, fat or thin, fit or out-of-shape—who can stand and get around can walk for exercise. Whether fast, slow, or somewhere in between, any mobile person can achieve health and fitness results that are nothing short of amazing, simply by walking.

While other activities have grabbed the headlines, walking has quietly become the most popular form of exercise in America. More than 60 million Americans now walk for exercise. Fitness experts and doctors recommend walking more than any other form of exercise. Clearly, walking for fitness is no passing fad.

Almost every week newspapers and magazines report new evidence that walking is good for us. It lowers the risk of heart attack, stroke, high blood pressure, diabetes, osteoporosis, and a long list of other serious diseases. Plus it just makes us feel better. No wonder legions of walkers are filling America's streets, tracks, and pathways. People are literally walking their way to better health.

To become healthier is reason enough to take up walking, but this is just the beginning. Walking can help produce another kind of fitness that is less obvious, less often discussed, but even more important: *spiritual* fitness.

Spiritual fitness is not a common term, but it should be. Our souls need nourishment and exercise every bit as much as do our bodies. Physical fitness can have a lifelong impact, but the impact of spiritual fitness can literally be eternal. Book stores and library shelves are well stocked with books about physical fitness, but spiritual fitness guides are harder to find. This book focuses on both.

Using walking to build both physical and spiritual fitness is a concept I stumbled across soon after I began exercising. "Walking with God" was a phrase I had heard all my life, but it took on new meaning when I put it into the exercise context. My daily exercise time became as much a time for reflection, prayer, and praise as it was a time for physical exertion. It was—and is—a private and personal time for building a one-to-one relationship with God, communing with God each day, and finding spiritual strength while also building physical strength.

The idea for writing this book came several years ago on one of my morning walks. I was striding along a quiet neighborhood street, watching the sun's first rays seep through a canopy of tall pine boughs. My thoughts drifted to a Scripture verse about new beginnings. I felt the exuberance of spirit that I so often feel when I combine physical and spiritual exercise. Simultaneously I was immersed in God's world and in His Word. It was the kind of feeling I wanted to bottle—a feeling too important not to be shared.

Walking with God is a simple idea that takes minimal effort, but the payoff is beyond measure. It is a way to build up both body and soul while attuning ourselves to the word and will of our Creator. It is—as every exercise program should be— preparation for abundant living. But in this case the abundance involves more than just good physical health.

Refreshed and renewed each day both in body and spirit, how can our lives fail to be richer, fuller, and more in accord with God's will?

*"Ask where the good way is, and walk in it."*
—Jeremiah 6:16

*Chapter One*

# Walking with God

*"Were not our hearts burning within us while he talked
with us on the road and opened the Scriptures to us?"*
*—Luke 24:32*

Jesus walked. From Judea to Samaria, Galilee to Syria, He walked. That was how people got around in the Holy Land two thousand years ago. Only the rich and powerful could afford chariots, and animals that could carry people were needed to haul freight. So people went from place to place on foot, regardless of the distance. Jesus did as others did. He walked.

Hiking from New York to Philadelphia would be unthinkable to most of us today, but such journeys—about one hundred miles—were routine in New Testament times. Jesus and His followers did not have the airplanes, buses, trains, and automobiles that we take for granted. And with no television, radio, or newspapers to help spread their message, they had to travel to reach people. Even for trips longer than the Pennsylvania turnpike—about the distance from Galilee to Jerusalem—they would simply lace up their sandals and walk.

It took days, sometimes weeks, for them to cover distances we now travel in hours. But this was not wasted time. Jesus used this time to teach His companions through stories and deeds. He often stopped to comfort, heal, and teach those He encountered along the way. Psychologists counsel us to spend "quality time" with the important people in our lives. Those journeys allowed for plenty of quality time.

The disciples must have been a curious bunch. The New Testament tells how Jesus answered many of their questions along the dusty roads of Palestine. Those answers form much of His message to us. We can only imagine the closeness and inspiration the disciples must have felt as they heard Jesus speak directly to them in prolonged, personal communication.

We may not be able to see and touch Jesus as they did, but we can still experience a closeness much akin to what the earliest disciples felt. Like them, we can walk with God, talking and listening, growing stronger in our faith and understanding. Walking still affords opportunities for sharing, just as it did two thousand years ago.

Whether in private meditation or in time spent with others, walking can provide a kind of time that is hard to find these days. This is time for uninterrupted focus, and what better focus can we have than our relationship with God? We no longer have to rely on walking to get us where we need to go, but we can rely on it to help get us where we need to be both physically and spiritually.

Walking for exercise produces health and fitness benefits too numerous and obvious to ignore. Study after study shows how it helps prevent disease, prolong life, and simply makes us feel better. And there are spiritual benefits, too. These may not be as obvious, but they are just as real.

Name a sport or exercise and you can find stacks of self-help books to tell you more than you really want to know about it. This is as true for walking as it is for golf, tennis, weight lifting, and scores of other activities. Those books usually focus only on the physical aspects of exercise. However, very little has been written about the spiritual benefits.

It is not that the spiritual, mental, and emotional effects of exercise are unknown. The scientific and medical communities have long recognized that exercise affects more than just our bodies. More than a decade ago, *The Physician and Sports Medicine* reported that more than 90 percent of physicians were prescribing exercise for patients with depression and anxiety. People simply feel better after exercise—happier and more positive.

Much of the credit for this increased sense of well-being during and after a good workout can be attributed to endorphins. These are chemicals our bodies produce and release into the bloodstream during exercise. Endorphins cause the "runner's high" that joggers often experience—an exuberant feeling that comes during and after a long, hard run. But endorphins are not just reserved for excessively strenuous exercise. Walking can also release endorphins into the bloodstream, and a "walker's high" is an equally enjoyable and attainable phenomenon.

Scientists have further explanations as to why exercise causes such good feelings. Some attribute it to the slight rise in body temperature that occurs during exercise. Others think it comes when the rhythm of steady exercise somehow connects with unexplained inner rhythms of the body. Whatever the reason, physical exercise makes us feel good and leaves us stronger, more at ease, and better able to handle the stresses of life.

Since exercise has such powerful effects on how we feel physically, mentally, and emotionally, it should not surprise us that it can produce spiritual benefits as well. Exercise can involve every part of our being, and we cheat ourselves if we do not plan and use our exercise time to improve every aspect of our fitness—body and soul.

Almost any exercise will do. It does not have to be as strenuous as running, swimming, or racquetball. Walking—the same activity that occupied so much of the early disciples' time—can still lead us to better physical and spiritual fitness. Not just walking, but walking with God.

##  Exercising the Body

We can avoid physical exercise, but we cannot escape its importance. Television, newspapers, and magazines bombard us every day with reminders that physical fitness can bring us healthier, longer lives. It is almost impossible to channel-surf without encountering an aerobic exercise workout, a TV "infomercial" for fold-away exercise equipment, or a news report on some new discovery of how fitness prevents serious illness. We are reminded daily that we should exercise.

According to a study published in *Walking* magazine, less than one-fourth of American adults exercise two or more times each week. Yet the 23 percent who do exercise report astounding results: less cancer; less heart disease; and lower death rates—to name a few of the big ones. Time spent exercising is a big investment in the future, and it pays very large dividends. But about 143 million of us simply ignore these facts, apparently hoping to beat the statistical odds.

> *"Be strong...all you who hope in the Lord."*
> *—Psalm 31:24*

Longer life should be reason enough to start exercising, but this is only where the list of benefits starts. Exercise increases our capacity for almost everything. Even something as simple as climbing stairs or playing tag with your children becomes easier after a few weeks of exercise. Exercise adds a spring to the step, and regular exercisers almost inevitably gain confidence in their ability to deal with the world around them. It not only affects the quantity of life, it improves the quality of living.

The effects of exercise sometimes show up in unexpected ways. For example, I have sung in church choirs since I was six years old, and I would never have thought walking could affect my voice. But my breath control for singing improved dramatically after I started exercising daily, a simple byproduct of my increased lung capacity. Our bodies are tools that we use in countless ways each day. If we take good care of them, they work more smoothly and improve our ability to handle the opportunities and demands of everyday life.

Though the benefits of exercise are clear and available to all, this whole subject has taken on an unfortunate air of complexity that scares some people away. With the exercise explosion, marketing experts have looked for—and found—ingenious ways to tap the pocketbooks of fitness seekers. The countless exercise-related products and constant bombardment of advertising can make the whole idea of exercising seem overwhelming.

Just look at athletic shoes. When I went out to buy a pair of sneakers twenty years ago, I usually found only two choices: high top or low cut. Today entire stores are devoted to athletic shoes, often charging astronomical prices. Some stores specialize in athletic shoes for women only, other stores in athletic shoes just for children. There are special shoes for walking, running, tennis, aerobics, cross training, soccer, and countless other activities. Something as simple as buying shoes has become a major production. But such complexity should not surprise us. It just shows what happens when adults take up activities previously done mostly by kids.

Until recent years the only persons you would likely see involved in neighborhood sports were children. Not so today. Drive through any suburb and you are likely to see adults walking, jogging, and riding bikes. Go to your local mall and you can usually spot older adults decked out in track shoes and athletic togs for "mall walking." Check out your nearest tennis courts and you will probably find more adults than children. Even the biggest couch potatoes you know are likely to say they plan to begin exercising but have just not started yet. The exercise trend has swept across our society like a tidal wave.

Fortunately, this trend brings rewards for everyone, not just for those who run fast, jump high, or want to turn every workout into an endurance contest. The rewards of physical exercise—better health, longer life, stronger bodies, and clearer minds—are available in low-intensity exercise as well as in high-intensity exercise. The same rewards are there, just with less exertion and fewer risks of injury. We do not have to be natural athletes or look like health spa models to enjoy all the benefits of exercise, and this is where walking comes in.

Walking is an exercise almost anyone can do. Except for the mobility-impaired, virtually all of us—young or old, agile or clumsy, muscular or weak—can walk. We begin walking somewhere around the end of our first year of life, and most of us continue for as long as we live. We may not have to rely on it for traveling long distances these days, but it still qualifies as humanity's main form of mobility.

Walking is our primary way of getting around, but it can be much more. It can be—and is—a highly efficient, highly effective form of exercise. Medical research has consistently shown that fitness walkers have better health and lower illness and death rates than people who are sedentary. Physicians recommend walking to their patients more than any other form of exercise, and many corporations are setting up special walking programs to help their employees become fit. Most experts on health and fitness now agree that walking is the best all-around exercise for most people.

Walking is also the most popular form of exercise in America. It may not be a sport that millions watch on Sunday afternoon television, but a National Center for Health Statistics survey showed that walking is the exercise of choice for about sixty million of Americans. It is also the exercise people stick to more than any other, and exercise will have lasting effects only if people keep at it. Studies show that walking has the lowest dropout rate of all exercises.

As people walk more, they get healthier. Physically active people live longer and have a better quality of life. They are stronger, are more vital, and have fewer illnesses to hold them back, their fitness warding off a variety of ailments from constipation to heart disease.

If it is hard to believe all these benefits can really come from something as simple as walking, read on. This is just the beginning.

 ## Exercising the Soul

Imagine the spiritual strength the disciples drew from walking hundreds of miles with Jesus—talking to Him, listening to Him, experiencing His presence every step of the way. They were among the most privileged people ever. No wonder they were so distraught when He was crucified, and so overwhelmed when He returned to walk with them again on the road to Emmaus.

The Gospel writers describe some of what it was like to walk with Jesus in those days. Luke tells of their "talking with each other about everything that happened" (Luke 24:14). Mark describes some of the conversations that took place, including one on the road to Jerusalem in which Jesus explained His coming death and resurrection (Mark 8:31). Matthew recounts how, on another trip, Jesus promised, "If you believe, you will receive whatever you ask for in prayer" (Matt. 21:22).

Many of the messages Jesus delivered while journeying with disciples form the foundation for our faith. Our individual journeys with Him today determine how we live out that faith. We can either heed His message, draw close to Him, and seek His will, or we can choose a different path. The Scriptures refer many times to this life choice as a "walk," and Christian living is frequently referred to as "walking" with God.

Walking is mentioned throughout the Bible. The Hebrew word for walk, *halak*, appears more than 1,550 times in the Old Testament. Similarly, the Greek word for walk, *peripateo*, is used repeatedly in the New Testament. Both words mean more than just physically moving. These words are used frequently to refer to a person's spiritual direction or lifestyle. Believers in the early church were often said to "walk in the light," "walk in the truth," or "walk in love and obedience."

*"I pray that you may enjoy good health and that all may go well with you, even as your soul is getting along well."*

*—3 John 2*

Walking has long been a metaphor for our spiritual lives. If we "walk with God," we are living in His presence, according to His will. If we "walk in the counsel of the ungodly," we live a lifestyle apart from God's will and commandments. This metaphor was perfect for biblical times, as walking was something early believers understood very well. People who journeyed hundreds of miles on foot could easily grasp the idea that walking with God means sharing highly personal time with Him over the long haul.

A close personal relationship with God is as important for Christians today as it was for the early believers. Obstacles too often rob us of the time we need and want to devote to enriching that relationship, but there are ways to find this time and create these opportunities. One of the best ways is to take literally this term used figuratively over two thousand years ago: *to walk with God*.

To live the Christian life—to walk daily with Him—takes the same kind of commitment and energy as physical exercise. Just as regular workouts build our physical bodies and make them stronger, spiritual exercise strengthens our faith.

It energizes us, enabling us to put our faith into action more vigorously. Without spiritual exercise our faith can atrophy like unused muscles, growing weaker and less able to make any difference in this desperately needy world.

Time is a great enemy of spiritual fitness. Most Christians would like to grow spiritually, but they never seem to have enough time. Competing priorities like jobs, families, even church activities rob us of the hours we might prefer to spend reflecting on Scripture, praying, and listening for God's guidance. For Bible study we too often snatch a quick verse from a calendar or devotional guide. For prayer we rely on brief moments in church or at mealtimes. Quiet time to listen for God's still, small voice is drowned out by noisy activities that, in the long run, are of very little importance.

Those who do find time to exercise the soul do it in a wide variety of ways. I know some who rise before daybreak to start each day with an hour or more of solitary devotional time. Others grab quiet time on lunch breaks or in the evening. Some even use commuting time for prayer and reflection, though my own experiences with freeway commuting have been far less than uplifting. The best time for one person might be impossible for another, but each person must find this kind of time. Spiritual fitness takes time and effort, just like its physical counterpart.

The similarities between spiritual fitness and physical fitness are striking. When we exercise our bodies by running or walking, we find ourselves running or walking more easily and effectively. If we exercise our souls by learning Scripture, praying, and reflecting on God's will, we find ourselves more often recalling His words, feeling His presence, and understanding His will. Basic exercise principles apply to both: it must be regular; it must be intense enough to accomplish its purpose; and it must be continued over a long period of time.

Most of us know persons whose good spiritual health is readily apparent. They may be dynamic pastors and Sunday School teachers or quiet, gentle folk who prefer the background, but they seem to have a special glow. Somehow, they seem to be in closer communion with God, more attuned to knowing and doing His will. Usually, the Christians who exude spiritual health simply follow through on their good intentions where many others do not. They do not just try to find time for spiritual matters, they make time. Although they may not call it a spiritual workout, they give study and prayer the same kind of priority that millions of others give to daily aerobics.

If you think you don't have enough hours in the day for both physical and spiritual fitness, think again. You can work on both simultaneously. Physical workouts vary in length from person to person, but experts agree they should last at least twenty minutes to have the desired impact. This is time in which the body is busy but the mind can roam freely. With planning and focus, you can use this time to mine a rich source of spiritual as well as physical strength. Those who choose to walk for fitness can turn it into a time for truly walking with God.

## A Personal Awakening

I am certainly not the first person to think of combining physical and spiritual fitness. I have talked with many others who use exercise time for prayer and reflection, from hard-charging fitness experts to slow-moving seniors. My own awakening to this idea came one year a few weeks before Easter.

I was out pounding the pavement around daybreak that spring morning when, out of the stillness, I began to hear the words and music of Handel's "Hallelujah Chorus." The only audible sounds were my footsteps and the occasional chirping of a waking bird, but the music was there, and I heard it. With each step I could feel the beat and hear the notes and words resound in my head as vividly as if they were being performed in a cathedral by a choir and full orchestra.

I do not know what caused that music to burst forth so wonderfully that morning. I had sung the piece many times, so maybe it was simply that I knew the music well. But it was different from just having a familiar tune run through my head. It was more majestic, more inspiring than any rendition I had ever heard, and I was overwhelmed by the reality of God's greatness and presence in the world around me.

As I moved briskly—the silent music resounding—praise began pouring forth. I began to thank God for everything I saw, and I felt a closeness to God that was truly overwhelming.

I returned home that morning highly energized. Management experts talk about the importance of feeling empowered, and I felt truly empowered by God that morning. I wanted to capture that feeling so I could immerse myself in it again and again.

Recreating a spontaneous "mountaintop experience" with God is not easy. Perhaps it is even impossible. But every Christian who has been to the mountaintop knows this desire to go back to feel that closeness once again. I wanted it the next morning when I set out to exercise again and was delighted to find it still there, waiting for my return. By focusing my thoughts and developing a pattern, I was able to turn what had been simply a time for physical exercise into a daily time for prolonged reflection, prayer, and praise.

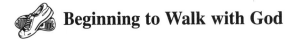

## Beginning to Walk with God

Anyone who exercises regularly knows how time-consuming it can be. In fact "not enough time" is the most common reason people give for not exercising at all. But anyone, regardless of how busy, can make time for exercise both physical and spiritual. This is one area of life in which it is truly possible to do two things at once.

My daily forty-five-minute walks add up to well over five hours each week, and these are hours I can put to more than one use. While the exercise only occupies my body, my brain is free to be focused on spiritual growth or, just as easily, to be left open for passing, idle thoughts. Since my "Hallelujah Chorus morning," I have found that with focus and commitment I can turn my daily fitness workouts into regular periods of walking with God.

Road maps are always useful in keeping us on the right path, whether hiking an unfamiliar trail or trying to build spiritual fitness. A guide of some sort is almost always essential. I have developed a guide that adds structure and focus to the spiritual dimension of my daily walks. I have found that with a little planning I can step out in the early morning mist with some Scripture verses, my prayer concerns, and matters to discuss with God all close at hand. For the next forty-five minutes or so, Jesus and I are alone on a dusty pathway, just as Jesus was alone with His disciples two thousand years ago. I end each journey stronger and more enriched from having been in His presence, enabled by His guidance.

Planning and effort are essential in any physical fitness program, and a little more of each can add a spiritual dimension. The time, place, equipment, goals, and even the activity itself all require prior planning. Rolling some preparation for one-to-one time with God into this process can produce a program that enhances both body and soul, giving new meaning to the term "total fitness."

Each person has different needs, so no two plans should necessarily be the same. Some folks begin exercising to take off weight, while others want to fight the impacts of specific diseases or just to feel stronger. Spiritually, some seek to build a fundamental relationship with God, while others try to strengthen specific aspects of their life and service. Our spiritual needs are just as diverse as our physical ones, but each of us can build an achievable plan to fulfill whatever those needs might be.

This book is about building a plan to meet your fitness goals, both physical and spiritual. It is not a book to be read and then put on a shelf to gather dust. It is designed for you to do something that you've always been taught not to do: write in it. Fill in the blanks as you follow each step to develop your own personal goals and game plan. Then use the tools in the last chapter for a spiritual tune-up during your first twelve weeks of walking. I hope that these chapters will become stepping stones in your personal pathway to physical and spiritual fitness.

Is it worth the effort? Absolutely! As an old Chinese proverb reminds us, a journey of a thousand miles begins with a single footstep. An eternity of walking with God can begin the same way.

*Chapter Two*

# Spiritual Fitness

*"If there is a natural body, there is also a spiritual body."*
*—1 Corinthians 15:44*

When we look in the mirror and see physical faults, most of us leave no stone unturned in trying to fix them. If it takes a crash diet, we start one. If it means exercise, we pull out the old gym shoes and get started. Physical shortcomings are easy to spot, and they usually get quick attention. Spiritual shortcomings are less visible, and they rarely get the same priority.

While we may be slow to turn a mirror on our spiritual lives, such neglect hurts the soul every bit as much as it does the body. Neglecting physical health allows the body to deteriorate and weaken, opening the door for disease. Neglecting spiritual health invites deterioration and weakness, too, but with the potential for far more devastating results. Working on physical fitness is important, but Jesus put the matter in perspective when He asked His disciples: "What good will it be for a man if he gains the whole world, yet forfeits his soul?" (Matt. 16:26).

Being spiritually out of shape is not uncommon, even among staunch Christians. Victims of this condition fill thousands of church pews every Sunday: good people who want and need to be closer to God but just are not managing to get there. From new Christians to lifelong believers, there is an aching need for better spiritual fitness.

Being a Christian involves belief, but living a committed Christian life involves much more. Outward symbols do not always mesh with inner feelings and commitment, as Jesus pointed out to the Pharisees two millennia ago. "Churchianity"—practicing the outward symbols but lacking the inner substance—is as common today as it was then, so we should not be distraught for feeling spiritually weak. Even David, whose faith was strong enough to challenge the giant Goliath, later found himself so spiritually out of shape that he begged God to "renew a right spirit" within him (Psalm 51:10 KJV).

Instilling, renewing, and sustaining a "right spirit" is the essence of spiritual fitness. It means knocking down obstacles that separate us from God, attuning ourselves to His will, and focusing our whole selves on living in right relationship with Him. This is no small order.

God is present in every aspect of our lives, but how we deal with His presence is up to us. We can ignore Him to the extent that He makes no difference at all, or we can cultivate His presence so that He becomes the focus of our every thought and deed. God will not intrude, but He is always there for us to include. He has left the choice to us.

The easiest choice is to simply avoid God. This way we do not have to worry about things like Bible study, prayer, and whether we are in step with His will. There are thousands of good excuses to rationalize this neglect. They may not hold much water, but they are almost as easy for us to believe as they are to find. Of course, these excuses only work when things are going well. When a crisis comes along and the chips are down, even those who have distanced themselves far from God tend to turn up the spiritual heat.

Spiritual fitness should be an everyday, lifetime pursuit for each believer. After all, Christianity is not a social club. It is a life-changing relationship—or at least it should be. Once we come to know Jesus in a personal way, we begin a whole new journey in life. We can never expect to know all we would like to know about God, at least not in this lifetime. But no one who honestly and earnestly gives Him center stage can avoid growing in faith and understanding. If we really want to know God's will, up close and personal, we can. The challenge is to truly desire this relationship, and to back up this desire with our time and energy.

Wanting spiritual fitness is easy; *getting it* is tougher. It takes commitment, self-awareness, lots of time, and plain old effort. For some, this is a natural outgrowth of finding God. For many, others it takes as much structure and persistence as trying to change from couch potato to athlete. Either way, it is well worth the effort.

Whether you are spiritually fit may be a question you have never asked yourself, but it is one that every Christian should be able to answer. If your relationship with God is so strong and personal that He is part of everything you think and do, you are probably in robust spiritual health. If not, you may want to take some positive steps toward better spiritual fitness.

##  Taking Stock

The first step toward spiritual fitness is getting a handle on where we already are. This sounds simple, but it requires something that is often quite difficult: honest self-evaluation, looking beneath our surface actions to focus on what we really think and feel.

Outward expressions of Christian living are important, but they do not always tell the whole story. Being in church every time the doors open does not guarantee a strong personal relationship with God. Differences between outward actions and inner commitment might fool our friends—maybe even our pastors—but they cannot fool God.

Some people seem to have such a strong personal relationship with God that they almost seem to glow. One of my old school teachers was like this. She did not push God in her classroom, and she did not need to. Her life was witness enough. She was as tough as nails on the academics, but she topped every "most admired" list and, many years later, is still the first teacher mentioned in reunion conversations. Quite simply, she had something special, and she knew how to make a difference in the lives of others by sharing her genuine Christian life with them. Her relationship with God clearly set her apart.

Such examples of spiritual fitness do not happen by accident. This teacher worked on her relationship with God seven days a week. Bible study was a daily habit, not a quick fix on Sunday, and she described her prayer life as being an endless conversation. God simply took top priority in her life, and this relationship influenced thousands of lives during her half-century of public school teaching.

Opposite examples are just as easy to find. Many Christians talk a good game but lack real spiritual depth—like one of my old college friends, a ministerial student with great talent but uncertain commitment. He could captivate a church congregation with his preaching on Sunday morning after a Saturday night of distinctly unpastorly escapades. He talked a great game but he lacked a foundation for his words. Perhaps this is why he ultimately abandoned the ministry for another career. Just showing up and looking the part on Sunday will not cut it in the long run. Robust spiritual health is not a one-stop, once-a-week deal.

Each of us fits somewhere on a spiritual health scale that runs from "badly out of shape" to "shining example." Unfortunately there are no neat scientific tests to pinpoint where we are on this scale. Computer models may be able to diagnose physical health with amazing accuracy, but there are no such devices to assess spiritual health. This is between each individual and God, so we have to use self-evaluation. And since God is the only other party involved, it had better be honest self-evaluation.

If our relationship with God is not as it should be, we know it. Others may not see it, and we may want to deny it, but we know it. Being distant from God simply feels different from being close. We may just need to take more time to think, pray, listen, and be quiet with the Lord. Or it may be something much bigger.

It is not unusual for Christians to have lingering questions about their relationship with God. Nor is it uncommon for those with great faith to feel inadequate in understanding God's Word and will. Each of us knows the strength of our basic beliefs, the priority we really give to God in our lives, and how willing we are to put feet to our faith. If we recognize the gaps that may exist between what is and what should be, we can confess these to ourselves and to God. This awareness and recognition is a big step toward a healthier spiritual relationship.

##  Nourishing the Soul

Spiritual health depends largely on what we put into our minds and hearts, just as physical health depends on what we put into our bodies. In the computer world, "GIGO" means "Garbage In = Garbage Out"—a reminder that computers can only produce good answers if they are fed good data. If garbage is all the machine has to work with, then garbage is all you can expect it to produce. The same is true for each of us.

If we constantly expose ourselves to garbage, we cannot expect God's light to shine through in our answers to life's daily problems. What goes into our minds and hearts has as much impact on our spiritual health as what goes into our bodies has on our physical health—maybe more. We all know that good physical health depends on good nutrition rather than a diet of fat, fried, and fast foods, yet we seem to think our souls can manage just fine with constant mistreatment.

Unfortunately, "fast food" for the soul is much easier to find than the good, nourishing stuff. Turn on a television around lunch time if you have any doubt. Millions tune in every day for soap operas, many of which are packed with more sex than is in the R-rated movies they refuse to attend. Millions more hang on every word of talk shows dealing with such common, everyday problems as "transvestite astronauts and their extraterrestrial love slaves." Books and magazines offer similar sleaze. Glance at the headlines on the tabloids lining your supermarket checkout counter to see how low publishers can stoop. Or for a real shock, peek into one of the steamy romance novels that have become standard fare for millions.

What we see, read, and hear stays with us. We may turn off the lights at night, but we cannot turn off the influences of the day. Spend an evening with a gory horror novel, a tense TV drama, or "killer rap" music, and these images will remain in your mind when the lights go out. Spend the same hours with a humorous book, a family-oriented television program, or some soothing music, and you will go to sleep with quite different images. We take in very little that does not leave an imprint, and *we* choose what will be imbedded in our minds.

We cannot and should not try to avoid everything that is unpleasant, distasteful, or controversial, but allowing ourselves to be overwhelmed by it is another matter. Anyone who believes offensive material goes "in one ear and out the other" is dead wrong. Where we focus our thoughts is a matter of choice, and we do not have to voluntarily consume garbage that drags our lives down. Maybe we cannot prevent it from being all around us, but we can prevent it from taking over our own minds and souls.

When I was a teenager a framed quote hung on the wall of my Sunday School classroom: "What you are to be, you are now becoming." This truth is not reserved for young people. Each of us, regardless of age, is what artists call a "work in progress." The brush strokes of each new day contribute to an ever-changing picture. Gradually, the canvas of life is filled in, but the finished work cannot be viewed until we have drawn our last breaths. Our continuous process of "becoming" depends on what we feed ourselves—mentally and spiritually—each day.

Spiritual anemia is widespread, and many of us invite it by substituting spiritual junk food for good spiritual nourishment. For example, the Bible is the best selling book of all time, and most American homes contain at least one copy. But millions of Bibles collect dust in the same homes where tabloids and romance novels get avid attention. The same is true with music. Most radio dials are set on rock or country stations that bombard listeners with messages of booze, sex, and drugs; while stations offering wonderful music, enlightening ideas, and reassuring messages too often score at the bottom of the ratings charts.

Escapist reading and popular songs can be as delightful as an occasional hot fudge sundae. But heaven help us if we make a steady diet of either indulgence without balancing it with more substantive stuff. If we let mental junk food crowd out what is spiritually nourishing, we suffer. As the Bible says: "Whatever is true, whatever is noble, whatever is right, whatever is pure, whatever is lovely, whatever is admirable—if anything is excellent or praiseworthy—think about such things" (Phil.4:8).

It is not enough to minimize our exposure to damaging influences; we must also make sure we get enough of the good kind. Good spiritual nourishment takes the same kind of desire, planning, and commitment as physical nourishment. Fortunately the steps are easy to manage:

- First, we must want it. If we are happy with our current spiritual condition and see no real need to improve it, half-hearted intentions will not help. To create change, we must truly want change. Visualizing something better and truly wanting it is an essential first step toward achieving it.

- Second, we must plan for it. We cannot expect to enjoy big improvements in our lives completely by chance. We may want to improve, but it takes more than desire to make it happen. The vision must be translated into specific actions, small steps that ultimately lead to great accomplishments.

- Third, we must work at it. No one expects to lose fifty pounds in one week, but almost any overweight person can expect to lose one pound each week for fifty weeks to accomplish this goal. This is not the easy way, but it is the realistic way. More important, it is the effective way. To borrow the words of early fitness advocate President Teddy Roosevelt, "It is only through labor and painful effort, by grim energy and resolute courage, that we move on to better things." The object here is to build a closer, more rewarding, personal relationship with God, and this is worth all the labor, effort, and courage we can muster.

Walking provides time that is perfectly suited for finding spiritual nourishment—extended time alone to focus our thoughts wherever we want them. For a half hour or more, without interruption, we can focus as easily on a subject that is substantive and inspirational as on one that is shallow and inconsequential. Focusing on God during brisk, daily walks is a way any person can get spiritual nourishment and build physical fitness at the same time. It is good for the body, and it is good for the soul.

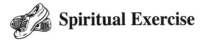 **Spiritual Exercise**

We do not grow by staying inactive, and spiritual exercise brings growth that is even more important than the physical kind. Muscles get stronger with each physical workout, and they power our bodies. Likewise, a person's relationship with God grows stronger with spiritual exercise, and this powers our very lives. While we look to barbells, aerobics classes, and other methods to work on physical strength, we cannot afford to shortchange that which continues long after our bodies have turned to dust.

 **Shaping Up: Belief**

"Ya Gotta Believe!" This slogan covered t-shirts, bumper stickers, and signboards all over New York during the summer of 1969. That city's "Miracle Mets" were making a run for baseball's World Series championship—their first ever—and Mets fans were far from shy about showing their support. Their belief in a team that had a long tradition of losing was rewarded when the Mets proved themselves the world's best. The loyal fans—the ones who had truly believed—responded with a celebration that still ranks among the biggest ever in a city known for its big celebrations.

We need something to believe in. Everyone does. For some it is a baseball team. For others it is a political party, family, religious group, or even show-business personalities. This is why more than twenty-five thousand people flock to Nashville each year to meet their favorite singers at the Country Music Fan Fair. It is why hundreds sleep outside locked gates to be at the front of early morning lines when Dallas Cowboys football tickets go on sale. It is why, day or night, you can find people kneeling on Hollywood sidewalks to place their hands in the cement handprints of movie stars.

Ralph Waldo Emerson wrote: "We are born believing. A man bears beliefs as a tree bears apples." The question is not *whether* we believe in something. We all do. The question is: *What* do we believe in?

Our beliefs largely determine how we live, and this is particularly true of religious beliefs. Devout followers of Islam construct each day around their three times for pausing to face Mecca and pray. Buddhists set aside time to meditate and recite mantras. And Hindus open and close their days with morning and evening adorations. These are all outward, visible expressions, and all religions have them—Christianity included. The beliefs behind our outward expressions, the beliefs we hold quietly and privately, have the greatest influence on how we live. These are the true foundation of our lives, whether we display them openly or simply hold them close in our hearts.

It is hard to live an exemplary Christian life without understanding why, so every Christian needs to understand just what he or she really believes. Just belonging to a church that adheres to certain creeds or doctrines is not enough. We need a solid grasp of our own personal beliefs. Otherwise, we can too easily veer from the path God has laid out specifically for us.

Getting a grip on our personal beliefs is as vital to spiritual fitness as a basic knowledge of physiology is to physical fitness. In each case the knowledge is a guide for the regular exercise it takes to get and stay in shape.

Basic Christian beliefs are essentially the same regardless of church or denomination. We often lose sight of this fact amid doctrinal debates and denominational differences. Outwardly, a Primitive Baptist church may seem to have little in common with a Russian Orthodox church, but both believe God exists, that He revealed Himself in Jesus, and that He continues to work in human lives through the Holy Spirit.

Perhaps it is a sign of God's greatness that He manifests Himself to different people in so many different ways. Jesus never confined Himself to the walls of a particular church, and no individual or denomination can limit the way He speaks to His people. This is evident in the diverse ways we live out our faith, with committed Christians standing on both sides of almost every emotional issue that arises. We may agree on little else, but we share the core beliefs of Christianity.

Christian faith is personal. This is how it starts, and this is how it continues. Accepting relationship with Jesus is a personal decision that no person, family, or church can make for anyone else. It has to be our own. Each of us must then apply this decision to everyday living in an equally personal way.

Thinking about our beliefs—our real, honest, personal beliefs—is an important part of spiritual exercise. When challenged by problems or temptations we need to be able to weigh each in relation to what we really believe. Much like a road map, our beliefs tell us which directions to take at critical forks in life's road. If we do not know our own beliefs, we are left with little help in knowing which way to turn. This is why regular reflection on our own beliefs is a key ingredient in spiritual exercise.

## Gaining Strength: Reflection

It is not enough for a Christian to just grasp basic beliefs and stop there. This would be stagnation. Growth is what we need. Although we should start out realizing that we can never learn enough to fully comprehend God, we can become fuller and more effective as we expand our knowledge and understanding.

Fortunately, Christianity comes with an instruction manual that has far more answers than we could ever have questions. Unfortunately, the instruction manual is so lengthy and complex that many hesitate to open it. At one thousand pages or more—depending on how it is printed—the Bible can be very intimidating. Yet it contains the knowledge and guidance we need to help us clarify, embrace, and live out our beliefs.

Taking the Bible in small bites is a great way to digest its meaning and refine our basic beliefs. Churches have known this for centuries, teaching Scripture to children one verse at a time. For millions of Christians, Bible knowledge consists

almost entirely of "memory verses" that they learned—one at a time, once a week
—in childhood Sunday school classes.

This small-dose approach is useful not just for children. Adults, too, often find
it easier to focus on one verse or chapter than to tackle the whole Bible at once.
This may partially explain why verse-a-day calendars have become so popular in
recent years. Long reflection on short passages is a good way to relate Scripture to
our lives personally. And making Scripture apply personally is what really matters.
Even atheists can be experts on what the Bible says, but opening up its life-changing
power requires getting personal.

To get spiritually fit, we must get into the instruction manual God has given us on
a regular basis. This can and should mean long, deep Bible study sessions; but it can
also mean focusing on just one verse until it becomes embedded in mind and spirit.

Using the bite-by-bite approach, it is amazing how much Scripture you can
digest. If you pick one verse each day to memorize, and you reflect on it while
walking for a half hour or more, you can learn a lot of Scripture in a very short time.
More important, you can have time to think about how it applies to you personally,
relating it to whatever might be your problems of the day.

There are countless methods for learning and reflecting on God's Word, but
few are as easy or effective as focusing on a Scripture verse while exercising each
day. In the time during a physical workout, we can learn, savor, and enjoy part of
the Bible's wisdom, letting it become part of us for the rest of our lives.

Using our exercise time this way follows the wisdom of an Old Testament
proverb: "A prudent man gives thought to his steps" (Prov. 14:15). What greater
thoughts could we give to our steps than the thoughts of God through His revealed
Word? And what better way to gain strength of faith and spirit for each day?

## Heavy Lifting: Prayer

Paul's charge to "pray without ceasing" (1 Thess. 5:17 KJV) may be the best spiritual fitness advice in the entire Bible. These words remind us that prayer should
be continual communication with God, not just something we resort to in crisis
situations.

Most people can walk or even run a fairly long distance if an emergency
requires it, but this does not necessarily mean they are physically fit. Adrenaline
kicks in when we face danger, and helps us through some situations we might not
otherwise survive. Winter travelers hike through miles of snow and ice when trapped
on impassable roads. Parents lift unliftable objects that fall on their children. Heroes

narrowly escape death while pulling others from burning cars or buildings. There are countless examples.

*"Therefore put on the full armor of God, so that when the day of evil comes, you may be able to stand your ground, and after you have done everything, to stand."*

*—Ephesians 6:13*

For many, prayer is the spiritual equivalent of adrenaline. It kicks in automatically in times of crisis—in a foxhole under fire, in a hospital when facing surgery, or in a car that is careening out of control. Prayers are uttered quickly and fervently when the chips are down, even by people who have never prayed before. Perhaps it is instinctive to call out to the Creator of life when all else fails, even for those who hold no conscious religious beliefs.

Adrenaline rushes and foxhole prayers may help us through a crisis, but we should never let them replace solid, physical, and day-to-day thoughts and actions that define who we are, what we believe, and where we place our priorities. If our beliefs define us as Christians, what higher priority should we have than staying in touch with the God we believe is alive and interested in our lives?

David had the right idea about prayer. You cannot read his psalms without getting involved in his continual interaction with God. Whether tending sheep while a humble shepherd or winning victories as King of Israel, he talked to God incessantly. He expressed thanks and praise with poetry and grace in his times of joy, and he cried out from the depths of his soul in times of despair. He argued and adored, but most of all he communicated without ceasing.

Compare this to how you communicate with God. You may pray as often, as comfortably, and as openly as David prayed, but such continual prayer is not the rule for most people. Even some very devout believers at times find it hard to pray. Perhaps it is because we feel inadequate to duplicate the style of fervent, flowery, public prayer we've heard in the church services of our childhood. Perhaps it is because we have not mastered the sixteenth century "thees" and "thous," but do not feel comfortable addressing God in everyday language. Perhaps it is because there is some obstruction in our lives, a wall we are unwilling to tear down so we can really talk openly with God.

Structured prayer can be wonderful, but mealtime blessings and bedtime prayers just barely scratch the surface. Meaningful communication comes in longer conversations, with time for listening as well as speaking. And, as with close friends, the conversations should be so frequent that we share virtually everything and anything that is important.

No subject is too large or too small when talking with God. Benjamin Franklin put it succinctly when he invoked the need for God's help with forming a new nation: "If a sparrow cannot fall to the ground without His notice, is it probable that an empire can rise without His aid?" From sparrows to empires, from our smallest problems to our largest joys, nothing is too large or too small to escape God's notice or merit God's concern.

*"Show me your faith without deeds, and I will show you my faith by what I do." —James 2:18*

Many of us have an amazing duplicity in our relationships with God. It is almost as if we think He will not know about something unless we tell Him, just as some churchgoers seem to think it is OK to sin as long as their pastor does not find out. If this were true, it would make God a pretty small god, and He put this idea to rest long ago. " 'Can anyone hide in secret places so that I cannot see him?' declares the LORD. 'Do not I fill heaven and earth?' " (Jer. 23:24). If we think it or do it, God knows about it. So why try to hide it?

Opening prayer up to all topics, conversing with God in the language of friends, and making prayer a continuing dialogue are all hallmarks of spiritual fitness. These practices indicate a willingness to include God in everyday living, not just keep Him around as an emergency button to be pushed in crisis or as a name to be dropped to impress friends.

This everyday aspect is to spiritual fitness, as regular, daily exercise is to physical fitness. It gives us the same power in daily living that others get only with a foxhole prayer or adrenaline rush. This brings the continual joy and confidence we need to make us fit for facing each of life's daily challenges.

It is as impossible to be spiritually fit without prayer as it is to be physically fit without exercise. Mahatma Gandhi said, "Prayer is the key of the morning and the bolt of the evening." If we use prayer to open ourselves to God each morning and to lock His love into our hearts each night, He becomes fully integrated into our lives. And when God becomes part of everything we think and do, we can feel the power of spiritual fitness surging within us. This does not mean we will never have moments of weakness, danger, or distress. But it does mean we can face these moments with the confidence that we are fit for any challenge.

## Practice: Being Witnesses

Some exercisers get involved in physical fitness for the sake of fitness itself. They do not plan any practical use for it, except perhaps to enjoy showing off their muscle definition and good looks. Some Christians seem to take a similar attitude toward spiritual fitness, but it does not work in quite the same way.

The ultimate results of physical and spiritual fitness are different. In physical fitness the outcome is the same regardless of motivation. You get the same health benefits no matter what drove you to begin exercising. You can have the most superficial reasons for doing it, and aerobic exercise will still lower your risk of heart attack and produce a long list of other health benefits. Spiritual fitness is totally different. You cannot really see the benefits until and unless you put your fitness to work.

The Bible is full of reminders that actions speak louder than words. Jesus said "Let your light shine before men, that they may see your good deeds" (Matt. 5:16). James wrote, "You see that a person is justified by what he does and not by faith alone" (James 2:24). Belief, faith, and prayer all go into spiritual fitness, but the fitness reaches its greatest level and purpose when it is put to work.

How we put our spiritual fitness to work—how we practice it in daily living—is something each of us must settle with God individually. It can mean a full-time commitment to some form of ministry, or it can mean just living so closely to God day-to-day that we positively glow. There are endless ways in which we can let our light shine in the corners of God's world that we occupy. Jesus set the example, and He said, simply and clearly, "Follow me" (Matt. 4:19).

Along with advertising slogans and a lot of pure trash, you can occasionally find a great philosophical nugget written on a T-shirt. One of my favorites is: "Practice Random Acts of Kindness." If Jesus were physically here today, wearing a T-shirt, I somehow think that might be one He would choose. It fits perfectly with His wish that we give food, drink, clothing, shelter, medical care, and other help to those who need it. As He reminded His disciples, "Whatever you did for one of the least of these brothers of mine, you did for me" (Matt. 25:40).

Doing something for "the least of these brothers of mine" is not always pleasant, and sometimes it means going out of our way. It is a lot easier to avoid Christian responsibility today than it was in New Testament times. Back then, everyone constantly intermingled, whether they were the sick, poor, and elderly, or the healthy, rich, and young. Today, the rich can avoid poor neighborhoods; healthy people can steer clear of hospitals and mental institutions; the young can easily congregate far from the elderly.

When we do not have to see the faces of those who need Christian compassion, we are not forced to become personally involved. This makes it easy not to worry about the less fortunate at all, or to salve whatever problem we have with our consciences by writing checks to homeless shelters, medical causes, or nursing homes. Many Christians have so embraced the institutional ways of helping others that they depend totally on the church to handle Christian witnessing instead of bothering with it themselves.

Many answers to human suffering lie in institutional aid, but not all. Random acts of kindness are essential. Even very small deeds can have very big impacts—a postcard to someone in a nursing home, for example, or a supportive telephone call to a coworker who has recently seemed depressed. Any of us can look around in the course of a day and see someone who needs a word of encouragement or a helping hand—a random act of kindness. Responding might not change the world, but it can change one small part of it.

We should not seek just to be spiritually fit, but to be spiritually fit *for* something. Otherwise, we will fall into a trap of self-centered spirituality that is no better now than it was for the Pharisees two thousand years ago.

Jesus did not *suggest* that we put feet to our faith; He *insisted* on it. As we submerge ourselves in God's will, which is inevitable as we grow closer to Him, we cannot avoid hearing His call to put our spiritual fitness into practice. Heeding this call and witnessing to what we have seen completes the process.

*Chapter Three*

# Spiritual Exercise

*"Therefore, strengthen your feeble arms and weak knees."*
*—Hebrews 12:12*

We can play at fitness with no trouble, but it takes effort to really get serious about it. This is why rowing, cycling, and stairstep machines are gathering dust in garages and attics across the US. It is also why athletic club memberships are often bought with enthusiasm, only to go unused after a few introductory visits. We usually begin a fitness program with great intentions; but great intentions are not enough to produce lasting results. To get real results requires exercise—months and even years of it.

Exercise and physical fitness have a cause-and-effect relationship: fitness comes as a direct result of regular, sustained, intense exercise. Your exercise cannot be haphazard if it is to be effective. It must be on a regular schedule and involve a continuing series of sessions, each lasting long enough to stretch your body's limits. This takes commitment. We are just kidding ourselves if we expect to be successful with a less serious approach.

The same cause-and-effect relationship exists between exercise and spiritual fitness. While we normally think of *exercise* in physical terms, the word does not apply just to activities in gyms, pools, and at playgrounds. Webster's *New Collegiate Dictionary* gives this definition of exercise: "to use repeatedly in order to strengthen or develop." This applies to lots more than just running and jumping. Singers use vocal exercises to develop their voice quality. Military units use training exercises to hone their fighting skills. Expectant mothers use breathing exercises to help them experience the miracle of natural childbirth.

Exercising the soul involves the same principles as exercising the body, and Webster's definition is right on target. If we "repeatedly use" our minds and hearts to focus on God, we cannot help but "strengthen" and "develop" our understanding, faith, and ability to communicate with Him.

Spiritual exercise leads to spiritual fitness just as physical exercise leads to physical fitness. This is as true as it is simple. To be truly effective, spiritual exercise requires every bit as much commitment and effort as good, hard physical exercise.

This does not mean that God pays attention only to those who wear out their knees on the prayer rug. He can answer split-second prayers, and a quick glance at a Scripture verse can have enormous impact. But there is no substitute for sustained time with God. Just as running each day will strengthen a person's ability to run faster, further, and longer; regular reflection and prayer will deepen one's understanding and strengthen one's faith. Best of all, it helps us feel closer to God.

Spiritual exercise incorporates the same basic principles as physical exercise, and these are very simple. Experts may differ on which physical exercises they prefer, but almost all agree that any exercise must include three characteristics to be effective:

- It must be done regularly.
- It must use the same muscles repetitively.
- It must be fairly intense.

 ## Regularity

Some people who do not think twice about running or playing tennis an hour each day will balk at the thought of devoting this much time to spiritual matters. They may want to feel closer to God, and they may genuinely want to find more time for prayer. But an hour a day? We can rationalize not having enough time for Bible study, reflection, and prayer. Maybe cloistered monks or nuns can fit these in, but squeezing it into our already overstuffed schedules is entirely different.

The activity trap holds most of us captive to an extent we neither realize nor want to admit. Activities related to our business, school, family, community, and even church increasingly rule our lives. Each one of these involvements begins with the promise of enhancing our lives, but then the activity itself seizes control.

Meetings, practices, games, performances, and other events start to seem mandatory instead of voluntary, crowding out what we really want and need to do.

When I moved to a new job several years ago, my family settled into a lovely suburban community in which, we quickly discovered, soccer was king. Scores of soccer fields dotted the town's greenbelts, and they never seemed to be empty. Almost every child old enough to walk was on a neighborhood team. And the parents were almost as involved as their kids, filling roles from coaches to caterers. Family schedules for the whole community revolved around practices, games, and booster-club meetings.

Many of our new friends had become involved in soccer for very sound reasons. Their children needed good exercise. Competitive sports teach important lessons about life and sportsmanship. And it is a wonderful way for children to have healthy interaction with others their age.

Unfortunately, a lot of folks lost sight of those sound reasons and got sidetracked by an entirely different emphasis: trophies and championships. For many, winning became everything. We began to see otherwise reasonable parents pushing their kids mercilessly. What started as a healthy outlet for family recreation became, for many of our neighbors, an activity trap that took priority over all else.

I realized our community's soccer mania was out of control when practices, games, and tournaments started to be scheduled for Sunday mornings. There was just not enough time during the week, organizers said. There weren't enough fields available to squeeze everyone in on Saturdays. When families were forced to choose between soccer and church, I was surprised by how many chose soccer. Many church-going families rationalized putting off church activities for a few months, with the assurance that they would start back after soccer season. I fear that too many children learned some very poor lessons about priorities along with whatever good lessons they picked up on those soccer fields.

Transient activities with little long-term value can easily crowd out the important things in life. We all have responsibilities we cannot avoid. Parents cannot suddenly opt for spur-of-the-moment fun instead of picking up their children after school, and commuters cannot succumb to the inevitable desire to avoid traffic by just skipping work. Teachers must teach, farmers must farm, builders must build, parents must parent.

Commitments and responsibilities are a fundamental reality of life, and we all have them. But they are not everything. Life offers a broad menu of choices. Once we satisfy the basics, each of us must decide where to place our highest priorities. Most Christians will quickly say that their relationship with God is at the top of their priority list. But actually working God into their schedules might be something different. After taking care of the basics—sleeping, eating, and working—most of us have few hours left in the day. And these quickly fill up with hobbies, family activities, television, and our need to just plain rest. We may know that we need more prayer, Bible study, and quiet meditation in our daily routines, and we may seriously want it, but it often winds up below laundry and toenail maintenance on our actual "to do" list. To follow the biblical mandate, we should probably tithe our time as well as our money. But I know few who could, or would, devote several hours a day to spiritual matters. The key is to set aside *some* time for those matters, and to make this a habit. Even a few minutes of spiritual exercise each day can yield enormous rewards. But finding time for God on a regular basis—like finding time for running or playing tennis—does not just happen. It takes a determined effort.

How and when to find time for spiritual exercise will not be the same for all of us. Far from it. My good friend who rises before five each morning for an hour or more of quiet devotion relishes this time with God. But I have another friend who thinks the A.M. side of the clock begins with eight or nine—definitely not an early riser. She saves her spiritual exercise for the opposite end of the day, with Scripture and prayer just before the lights go out at night. There is a great inner peace that comes with having Scripture verses linger in your mind as you drift off to sleep. Both of these vastly different approaches lead to the same result: an everyday habit of spiritual exercise.

Like most people these days, I once fell victim to the activity trap by letting my schedule become impossibly crowded. At one point I was working twelve-hour days and taking on more church and civic responsibilities than good sense would suggest. The result was a constant round of meetings, appointments, and other events that threatened the "quality time" I needed with my family. I felt like a hamster running full speed on a cage wheel.

I might have been tempted to shortchange God and squeeze Him out of such hectic days if another concern had not come into play. Perhaps to keep up my hectic pace or perhaps because of my age, I realized my physical condition needed more attention. So I started exercising. I quickly discovered that I didn't have to leave God behind when I left home for my daily workouts.

Soon after I began running and walking for physical fitness, I began to use that daily half-hour or more to focus on spiritual matters. The physical exercise produced the desired fitness results and was very satisfying; but it was the spiritual dimension that ultimately became more dominant and fulfilling. In fact, the spiritual aspects of my daily exercise became my prime focus, with the physical part taking a secondary role. This spiritual exercise has become the foundation for everything else I do, making me more fit to handle other challenges.

For exercise, mornings have always worked best for me. It is purely a personal choice, but I like the feeling it gives me at the start of the day. I also avoid spending extra time in the locker-room by getting the exercise over before I shower and dress for the business day. Through several particularly hectic years, this meant slipping into my athletic togs and hitting the streets by about 4:15 A.M. so I could be finished in time to commute from the suburbs and be at my desk in the city by 6:30 A.M. Whether there was snow on the ground or the pavement was warm from the early morning sun, I would step off into the morning darkness for a brisk three miles.

But I was not alone. I began each of those very long days with God, focusing on a portion of His Word and enjoying uninterrupted conversation with Him. This fortified me through several years of a schedule that I now realize was excessive. It still fortifies me each day, but now at a saner, more civilized hour!

*"Do not conform any longer to the pattern of this world, but be transformed by the renewing of your mind. Then you will be able to test and approve what God's will is—his good, pleasing and perfect will."*
*—Romans 12:2*

Regular exercise is the key to building fitness, whether physical or spiritual, and walking with God is an easy exercise habit to establish. Walking is so easy that there are no good reasons *not* do it. It does not require special training, equipment, or facilities. It can be done in your neighborhood or in a nearby shopping mall as easily as on a special track. It can be done at any speed—it is not just for the young, strong, and agile. Anyone can reap the physical benefits with just a little determination.

You can also reap spiritual benefits by using this time to focus on God. A brisk walk of a half-hour or more several days each week creates a personal quiet time that is perfect for communing with God. It does not require getting up earlier or eliminating other activities, and it precludes the possibility of being interrupted by telephone or visitors. Walking allows your mind to roam freely. To add a spiritual dimension to your exercise is just a matter of focusing your thoughts.

God is with us all the time. He is there when we are walking, whether or not we pay attention to Him. He will not intrude, however; it is up to us to recognize

His presence and invite the personal communion that is always available. So the concept of "walking with God" is really quite simple. It is just a matter of removing a mental veil,
inviting God to join you, and communicating with Him one-to-one.

To focus regularly on God should be among our highest priorities. Prayer and reflection help us temporarily close out the world and open ourselves to God's Word and will. When this becomes a regular part of life—truly a habit—we find ourselves becoming closer to our Creator and we view ourselves more consistently in His terms instead of our own.

 ## Repetition

To produce noticeable results, any exercise must be repeated and repeated and repeated. Weight-lifters use the number of "reps" they can perform as a yardstick to measure their gains in strength. Aerobic dancers repeat steps over and over to build up specific muscles. Tennis pros develop their smooth, consistent strokes by hitting ball after ball after ball—thousands of them. Whether in darts or decathlon, repetition is a key to success.

It is a matter of patterning. Repeating the same physical movements over and over causes muscles to develop habit patterns. The movements become easier as those patterns become routine. Habits are nothing more than patterns of behavior, and our habits have an enormous effect on how we perform—spiritually as well as physically. We build habits and create patterns simply by doing the things we do. Good or bad, we develop patterns by repetition.

The concept is easy to see in physical terms. Take the golf swing, for example. How a golfer moves his arms, legs, hips, head, shoulders, feet, and hands all affect the swing and where the ball will go. Pull the head up too fast while swinging, and the golf club will "top" the ball, causing it to roll only a short distance. Keep the right shoulder too high on the downswing, and the club head will hit the ball too far outside, causing the ball to "slice" to the right.

It takes hours on the practice tee to get every part of the body working right on every shot. Every muscle that comes into play must develop a pattern of movement— a habit. If all the habits are good and work together just right, the result is a "grooved swing" that looks and feels the same every time. This kind of swing is the goal of all serious golfers, and it takes constant attention to keep it as well as to get it. Even the most successful professionals still hit hundreds of practice balls each week. They know that a grooved swing can only be built and maintained through repetition.

In spiritual matters, the idea of forming habit patterns through repetition has bad connotations for some Christians. To some, repetition means perfunctory prayers, half-hearted creeds, and putting symbolism before substance. But repetition is no stranger to the church, nor should it be. All orthodox Christian churches repeat certain words, actions, and patterns of worship—the Lord's Prayer and communion, for example.

To repeatedly do, say, and reflect on certain words and activities can strengthen our faith, just as repeating physical movements can strengthen our bodies. The words and actions should never become an end unto themselves; but neither should they be shunned as irrelevant. These rituals have been given to us by God to help deepen our understanding and draw us closer to God—goals worthy of every Christian's effort.

Using repetition to strengthen faith perfectly matches the definition of *exercise*. Each prayer, meditation, and Bible study helps build our ability as Christians, just as each repetition of a golf swing or weight lift helps build a physical ability. If we repeatedly pray, meditate, and study God's Word, these activities begin to come more easily and naturally. More important, they produce a spiritual "grooved swing." Our words, thoughts, and actions combine to create something far greater than the individual parts.

Wouldn't it be wonderful to find intense, continuing closeness with God in an instant? Perhaps some are fortunate enough to have this blessing. But most of us are more likely to feel closer to God by doing things that focus our attention on Him: searching the Scriptures, praying, and listening for Him. This is spiritual exercise, and most of us need lots of it. The more often we repeat it, the better and more effective it becomes.

To use repetition in our quest for spiritual fitness is not a new idea. The Bible tells us to pray continually (1 Thess. 5:17) and to continually offer to God a sacrifice of praise (Heb. 13:15). From Genesis to Revelation we see that separating ourselves from God leads to desolation, and that faith, understanding, and closeness to God come when we seek Him and listen for His voice. We know what we should do. Our task is to "continue in what [we] have learned" (2 Tim. 3:14). And we should do this repeatedly.

There is no "one-size-fits-all" approach to the repetition of spiritual exercise. How we handle this is up to us. But we should approach it as we would approach physical exercise—picking a method that works best in our own lives. Prayer, praise, and meditation can take countless forms. What works for one person may not work for another. Whether in daybreak devotionals, a quiet time at noon, or late-evening walks, everyone needs a time, place, and method to focus on God without interruption or distraction. The point of this book is to help you learn how to combine the repetition of spiritual meditation with the repetition of the easy, effective physical exercise of walking.

Most new exercise programs make us feel awkward at first. They involve doing something new, and most of us rediscover long-forgotten muscles when we start out. In brisk walking, for example, our leg muscles are often the quickest to jolt our consciousness. If they have not been used regularly, they tend to be a little sore after the first few long walks. This soreness passes quickly, though, as these muscles gain the strength they need to handle the new demands. Lungs that cannot gasp enough air during our first brisk walks quickly gain the capacity to handle greater speeds and distance. Hearts that start out beating like jungle drums soon pump more blood with fewer beats per minute. With repeated exercise the whole body grows stronger and more efficient even in the low-stress activity of walking.

Using physical exercise as a time for spiritual growth takes a similar adjustment. In the beginning it may seem awkward to launch into silent prayer while striding around a track or through the corridors of a shopping mall. But this initial awkwardness disappears quickly and is soon replaced by relaxed efficiency.

The more we pray, the better we pray—whether on our knees or on the road. Many who pray every day in private feel different when called on to pray in public. But just as praying openly in a Sunday school class or Bible-study group begins to feel natural after a few times, so does prayer on the move.

We simply get better at things by doing them again and again. As each repetition makes an activity seem easier and more natural, we become more comfortable. Just as walking every day enables us to walk farther and longer, having one-to-one time with God every day cements His presence in our lives much more than just calling on Him occasionally.

Communicating with God is as essential to Christian living as communicating with a spouse is to a successful marriage. No one would expect to build a close, loving marital relationship by speaking only once a week, and no one should expect to build a close relationship with God by giving Him only an hour each Sunday. Loving relationships call for sharing, and no one is more able, willing, and available to share in our lives than God. We must take advantage of His willingness.

Spiritual exercise while walking may feel odd, even uncomfortable, at first. But repetition makes any difficulty fade rapidly. In its place comes a comfortable naturalness as we train and strengthen ourselves both physically and spiritually. As the Scripture says, "A man reaps what he sows" (Gal. 6:7). The more effort we put in, the more benefits we reap, whether walking alone or walking with God.

**Intensity**

Watch a weight-lifter's face as he strains under a bar loaded with several hundred pounds of lead. Or watch the face of a professional tennis player as she throws her whole body into a hard serve. Great athletic accomplishments take intensity, and great athletes must focus themselves totally to get peak performance from every muscle in the right way at the right time. The intense physical and emotional energy shows in their faces as well as in their rippling muscles.

*"Do not be deceived; God cannot be mocked. A man reaps what he sows."*

*—Galatians 6:7*

No athlete becomes great without intensity. Natural talent alone simply will not do it. From thousands of hours of conditioning and practice to crucial split seconds in championship competition, the winners are those who intensely focus both on effort and outcome. They have the same personal concerns as everyone else, but they are able to temporarily shut these out to focus on the tasks at hand.

Most of us can have effective and satisfying physical exercise with far less intensity than is required of professional athletes. Weekend tennis players can get superb workouts with a small fraction of the intensity needed to win at Wimbledon, and exercise walkers can strengthen muscles and burn calories with far less intensity than is needed for Olympic race-walking. Still, a certain level of intensity is required. Even amateur athletes must press their own limits to make real gains in strength or ability.

At any level, our exercise— whether physical or spiritual—must be focused and intense to produce results. Without intensity in spiritual exercise, there is little chance of strengthening faith or improving one's capacity for Christian service. Such results do not happen by chance, any more than running a four-minute mile happens by chance. The potential may be there, but it takes intense spiritual exercise to develop it.

The type and amount of intensity needed will vary from person to person, whether in physical or spiritual exercise. No one would suggest that a seventy-year-old walker use the same training methods as a nineteen-year-old old football player. Nor should a lifelong Bible student approach spiritual exercise in exactly the same way as a new Christian. In all cases, though, the intensity can be measured in two ways: time and focus.

## Time

Each exercise session must last long enough to be effective. Most experts recommend at least twenty to thirty minutes for aerobic exercise. Golfers should allot at least this much time for sessions on the practice tee. Marathon runners use well-planned schedules of daily times and distances as they build up for a big race. Without devoting sufficient time to any physical exercise, few would really expect to reap much benefit. Why should we expect spiritual exercise to be any different?

Time management is critical in our hectic world, as a parade of priorities compete for our severely limited time. We have to be able to separate the big things from the small ones, recognizing that certain priorities are most important and making time for them. Some very busy people, for example, are careful to schedule "quality time" with their children, while forgetting that quality is not the only critical factor. Quantity matters, too. We cannot expect to build solid parent-child relationships in a couple of half-hour sessions each week. And we cannot expect to build a strong relationship with God if we only catch Him briefly from time to time.

When and where to communicate with God is an individual choice, but devoting sufficient time is vital. God is too important for superficial treatment, and it is hard to get beyond superficiality in a quick prayer or a thirty-second meditation over our morning corn flakes. Our time with God should always be "quality time," but we should never shortchange the quantity. If we do, we are the losers.

Walking with God is an easy way to set aside time with God that meets both the quality and quantity requirements. As for quantity, physical exercise sessions should last at least twenty to thirty minutes. As for quality, the very nature of walking ensures that the time can be private, shared only by you and God.

## Focus

To set the time aside is half the battle; the other half is using this time effectively. This takes focus—something I had trouble with when I began to combine spiritual meditation and physical exercise. I would start out with good intentions to pray and meditate, but my mind would wander. My mind would drift to planning my day, calculating an expected expense, or dwelling on some family or business problem. I needed something to help open my heart's door to God as I began each session and to keep it from easing shut after a few minutes.

The solution I found was simply to jot a verse or thought onto a card and carry it with me, pulling it out and re-reading it occasionally to keep my focus throughout the walk. This practice plants an inspirational nugget in my mind before I step out the door and then helps me keep it there. Paul advised, "Let the word of the Lord dwell in you richly" (Col. 3:16). This Word can bless richly in small doses as well as large. A short verse or an especially meaningful quote can stimulate thought and set the stage for prayer, whether in church or walking down a country lane.

Walking is not a time for in-depth Bible study, nor should it be a substitute. But it provides a unique opportunity to focus on an enriching thought. Reading a few lines just before stepping out implants that thought in your mind. Carrying it along on a card for several more readings along the path is even better, reinforcing the message and often helping you commit it to memory.

As you think about a powerful nugget of Scripture through a half-hour or so of walking, it becomes a part of you. Dwelling on it at length and considering how it applies personally imbeds the thought in your mind so deeply that it lingers long after you have shed your walking shoes and gone on with other events of the day.

This is nourishment for the soul. It may not be a banquet-sized helping of Scripture and study, but some of life's tastiest morsels are best when savored in small bites. You may even find that, like good appetizers, these delicious moments whet the appetite for more. Most important, it is so simple and easy that it should not intimidate anyone into avoiding it. The ease and convenience of walking make more people stick with it than with any other exercise, and this approach to spiritual nourishment offers precisely the same ease and convenience.

Like walking itself, the ease and pleasure of "walking with God" keeps us coming back for more, and this is no small factor. Success in any fitness program—physical or spiritual—depends on our keeping at it.

With time and focus you will find it comfortable and fulfilling to step off for a walk, saying as you start out, "Good morning, God," and beginning a conversation so personal that it will become the highlight of your day.

*Chapter Four*

# Walking Alone with God

*And He walks with me,*
*And He talks with me,*
*And He tells me I am His own,*
*And the joy we share as we tarry there*
*None other has ever known.*

—*"In the Garden" by C. Austin Miles*

Time alone is special, and it seems increasingly hard to come by these days. Family and job commitments, school and church activities, community and charity involvements all conspire to rob us of time we need for being quiet, for thinking, for simply being alone. Some need solitary time more than others, but everyone needs it to some extent.

*Needing* time alone can be far different from *having* time alone. Time is one of the rarest commodities for most of us. How can we carve out a part of each day—or at least a few parts of each week—when we have so many competing priorities? One way is to get serious about walking for exercise, making walking a regular part of our daily and weekly schedules. It is certainly not the only activity one can enjoy in solitude, but it is one that is easy to justify to ourselves and to others.

With the need for exercise so universally understood, no one blinks an eyelash when a friend, coworker, or family member sets aside an hour or so each day to run, walk, or visit the gym. This is one chance to be alone that most people can actually take beyond the "this is something I should do" phase. Why not set aside some time for exercise, and enjoy the luxury of spending a little time alone?

*"Yet I am not alone, for my Father is with me."*

*—John 16:32*

The word *alone* is a relative term, of course. God is with us wherever we go and in whatever we do, and who would want it any other way? One of the best parts of being alone can be the opportunity to get beyond the clutter and clatter of daily life that comes between us and the realization of God's presence. Time alone is time we can use to answer His call: "Be still, and know that I am God" (Psalm 46:10).

Every summer during my teen years I spent a week or two at a mountaintop religious conference center that contained a quiet, rustic prayer garden. Some of my most meaningful moments at those conferences were those I spent alone with God in that garden. It was a small place—just a few benches scattered among trees and bushes—yet it seemed a million miles away from the rest of the world. God was there, and I could feel His presence each time I went there to sit, think, and pray.

God is everywhere, of course. I did not leave Him behind when I walked out of that garden, special though it was. He did not confine Himself to that small patch of ground, awaiting the possibility that I might drop by again. These times and places, though, lend themselves to helping us feel God's presence. Somehow we focus on Him more easily in a prayer garden than in an office building or shopping mall. Though we can be alone with God anywhere and anytime, it requires focusing *our* attention, not His.

When I discovered the joy of walking with God, it was almost like returning to that mountaintop prayer garden. But this time it was not a place I could just visit occasionally. It was a way I could experience true closeness with God every day, whether at home or on the other side of the globe.

The whole idea of walking with God is to use one's exercise walking to focus on and communicate with Him. This means connecting with God mentally and emotionally at the beginning of each walk. It means staying focused on Him instead of letting one's mind drift after the first few minutes. It means concentrating from beginning to end on sharing your concerns with Him and listening for His voice.

 **Creating Closeness in Solitude**

For me, there are three elements that flow very naturally in a quiet walk with God: reflection, prayer, and praise. If this sounds like a worship service, maybe it is.

A good walk centered on God can be as meaningful a worship experience as any you might experience inside a church. Not that it should replace church attendance; but there is something very special about worshiping God alone in the beauty of His world while caring for the miraculous human body He has created.

##  Reflection

I like to begin my walks in reflection, thinking about a Bible verse or quotation that helps me focus on God. I read over whatever I have chosen, then try to internalize it, memorize it, and make it mine.

An old story tells of a school teacher who encouraged her students to memorize their work. "Repeat something ten times and it will be yours forever," she said. Pausing, she heard a girl on the back row quietly repeating, "Alan, Alan, Alan…" I doubt that this really works as a way to land a sweetheart, but the basic principle makes sense. If we memorize something, it becomes ours forever. And if that something is Scripture, it is ours to use in witnessing to others as well as a vehicle for hearing God's voice.

As I get farther along my walking route, I try to take the verse or quote apart and think about its meaning—not only in its original context but how it applies to me in specific situations. For example, it is useful to understand the circumstances surrounding the prophet Elijah's words about how people violated God's commandments by making and worshiping idols (2 Kings 17:16). But it is far *more* useful to consider how I might have idols every day—money, job, activities—that separate me from God. Such personal application of Scripture can be truly life-changing.

Just as a Scripture text gives structure for a pastor's sermon, a focus thought gives structure for the spiritual aspect of my walk. If I stray far from it, I pull out the card on which I have written it and read it again. Focusing on God is like tuning into a radio station: It helps me to get on the right wave length.

## Prayer

Prayer comes naturally after a period of reflection. I find it hard to think very long about God and about my relationship with Him without wanting to talk with Him. Using this verse from 2 Kings, for example, I might very naturally begin talking to God about the idols I have created that separate me from Him, recognizing them and asking His help in tearing them down so I can find closer relationship with Him.

This is a beginning, and prayer seems to flow very naturally after this. It is similar to what is going on in the physical part of a walking session—getting beyond the warm-up phase and up to full speed in my direct communication with God.

I like to pray aloud when walking alone. This is why I usually choose a quiet, out-of-the-way place to walk. Others, seeing me talking away with no one else around, might think I'm nuts. This option is not always available, but whether aloud or with a quiet, inner voice, prayer while walking usually is—and should be—from the soul. It is for communication with God, not for show. And this communication can cover anything. Nothing is off limits when we are alone with God, talking directly to Him.

Prayer reminders are helpful, so I like to carry them along as well. As I write these words, for example, a close family friend is undergoing surgery. Her name was at the top of my prayer list when I headed out for this morning's walk. Such reminders are just the beginning, however. Other prayer concerns seem to bubble up like spring water during a long walk. Praying for one person is very often a reminder of others as my heart begins to open up.

You cannot jot down everything on a prayer list. Intense, prolonged prayer leads to discussions with God about people and events we might never think of planning for in advance. This is one of the beauties of the experience. Once you start walking with God, intensely personal and meaningful discussions can occupy most of the time you are at full exercise stride.

 **Praise**

Following your time of reflection and prayer, praise flows almost inevitably. After thinking about God's Word and will, then praying for guidance and help, it is natural to feel so close to God that you want to express awe, thanks, and love. This, in a word, is *praise*.

Sometimes as I draw toward the close of a long walk with God, a hymn or praise song will begin playing through my mind. Often it will contain words related to what I have just been discussing with God. At other times it will be simply a love song, reminding me of God's boundless love or expressing my love for the One who cares enough to truly never let me walk alone. Having learned hymns as a child, I am now blessed when the words of old hymns come back to me in strange and unexpected ways. They bring me quiet reassurance when I am under stress, and are a marvelous vehicle for praise—whether sung aloud in church or remembered quietly toward the end of a long walk.

As prayer and praise are intertwined, we may not know where one ends and the other begins. After prayer for ourselves, others, and events or concerns of the world, it somehow seems natural to continue speaking to God in thankfulness and love. What better way to end a long walk? It gives a sense of completion and helps one begin the day's activities with a sense of fullness and exhilaration.

Through all of these phases—reflection, prayer, and praise—I try to continually focus back on whatever verse or thought I used at the beginning of my walk. This provides the framework for all the rest, and helps me think of things I might not otherwise consider, opening me up to God's voice in a new way every day.

Finding good material is easy. Sometimes I just open the Bible, read the first verse I see, and memorize it before walking out the door. Sometimes I look back at an old church bulletin, drawing thoughts from the pastor's sermon, a line from a hymn that was sung, or some other reminder from the previous Sunday. And sometimes I run across a book that is a real treasure-trove of inspirational nuggets.

One such resource appeared several years ago in the form of a verse-a-day Bible calendar that I received as a Christmas gift. I began pulling off the top sheet of the calendar each morning, tucking it into my pocket, and reading it as I walked down the street. Not only did it give me a thought for starting out, but I could pull it out to read again if my thoughts wandered. And since they were not always familiar verses, I found I was memorizing Bible passages I had not known before. Most important, though, focusing on one verse for a half-hour or more took me further beneath the surface of Scripture than I had gone before. I had time to reflect on the nuances, think of how it applied to my own life, and use it as a springboard to pray about concerns that might otherwise have escaped me.

 ## Walking Cards

After using that calendar, I decided to stick with the basic concept but design my own, tailoring it to what I really needed for my daily walks. I wanted good focus thoughts, but I needed more. I needed a way to scribble prayer reminders to take with me and to jot down ideas for follow-up after I returned. And since I had also started keeping a daily walking log—to keep track of the dates, places, distances, and times of my walks—I was soon dealing with several pieces of paper before, during, and after each walk. I needed something that could combine all those functions, so I came up with the "walking card." This gives me a place to combine several functions into one easy-to-use format.

The most important advantage of a walking card is portability. Like the verse-a-day calendar sheets I used at first, the cards are easy to tuck into my pocket or waistband. They are also stiff enough that they do not blow around when I pull them out to read along the trail, even on breezy days. They are a perfect size, with enough space for all the information I need, but not so bulky that they are hard to manage. As an added benefit, they are easy to file for future reference.

Here is the design I use:

(front side)

# Walking with God

**Thought for the Walk**

*"Love your enemies, and pray for those who persecute you" (Matt. 5:44 NIV).*

**Prayer Concerns**

_____

_____

_____

_____

_____

(back side)

**Date/Place** [                /                ]

**Distance/Duration** [    .    *miles* /    *minutes*    *seconds* ]

**To Do:** (ways to follow up on thoughts from today's walk)

_____

_____

**Special Notes:** (observations or inspirations from the walk)

_____

_____

_____

There is nothing magic about my design for walking cards. You might want to add or subtract some elements. I have boiled it down to four basic parts that work best for me: focus thought, prayer list, follow-up planner, and data about each walk.

## *Focus Thoughts*

The focus thought works very much like a diver's springboard. It supports me as I step out, then it propels me on to something more complex. Unlike the diver, however, I can return to it as often as needed to regain my footing in the midst of the activity.

I have used all kinds of sources for my focus thoughts—Bible verses, quotes, hymn lyrics, sermon themes, and whatever else strikes me as a worthwhile topic for conversing with God. Over time, however, I have come to rely almost entirely on Scripture. There is so much between the Bible's covers that can be applied to daily living, and I like to dwell at length on those messages in small bites.

Finding which small bites to take with me requires a bit of work, but there are shortcuts. The easiest way is to simply take a Bible and a stack of file cards, then copy a verse onto each card. Some Bible passages lend themselves more to study within context, but thousands have relevant meaning even when standing alone. It is not difficult to recognize which passages will make good focus thoughts and which will not.

The verse-a-day calendars that are now so common in Christian book stores are easy sources, too, whether you just tear off a page each day, as I did in the beginning, or copy their content onto your own walking cards. Devotional books also contain good, short verses. I include some good verses—enough for twelve weeks of walking—at the end of this book to help you get started.

Whatever your source for focus thoughts, choose ones with two key elements: meaningful content and brevity. Each focus thought should have enough substance to lead into meaningful reflection and prayer, but it should be brief enough to prevent your stumbling along the trail as you read it.

When I head out to walk each morning, I pick up my walking card for the day and read the focus thought as I walk out to my starting point. Then I tuck the card into my pocket or waistband and work on memorizing the verse while stretching and warming up. As I go over the words in my mind, I begin thinking about what they mean to me personally. This usually comes by the time I have started walking and am picking up my pace. By the time I reach full stride and am moving briskly down the trail, I am talking with God about the words, phrases, meanings, and implications. I have bounced off the springboard into full communication with God.

## Prayer List

Years ago, when my father was hospitalized for the first of several cancer surgeries, many friends sent cards in which they wrote that they were praying for him. He was deeply touched to know that others were concerned enough about him to come before God directly on his behalf. Years later I came to understand this, myself. When I was facing the most difficult circumstances I had ever encountered, my family and I were blessed by the assurances of prayers not only by friends but by people we had never even met. It was humbling, and more reassuring than I can begin to describe. Prayer works, and part of any Christian's life should be prayer for others. There are books full of advice on how to remember who and what to include in one's prayer. Some suggest going down the alphabet to remember people whose names begin with A, B, C, and the rest. Others recommend word-association techniques, such as remembering to pray for Mr. Oaks whenever you see an oak tree. Whatever system you use, praying for others is an invaluable gift of Christian love.

I use lists. I use them for daily "to do" items and I use them as prayer reminders. Prayer lists help me remember what I want to talk about with God, from asking to thanking. They include people, events, and other concerns I might have, some perhaps as odd as others are common. Just as we discuss the concerns of our heart with good friends, God invites us to share our concerns with Him. So my walking card includes room for a prayer list, and I suggest that you use one, too.

If you carry a walking card in your pocket or purse and jot down names and ideas as they come to you during the day, you will have a ready reference when you start out to exercise. This helps prevent forgetting or overlooking important prayer concerns. Then as you begin communicating with God on your next walk, you can pull out the card to recall those items you wanted to take to Him, whether you are sharing, asking, or thanking.

The prayer list on a walking card does not need to be long. A word or line can capture the main concerns of your heart on any particular day, and there will be new ones each day. Keeping track of these is easy if you write them down, helping make intercessory prayer a daily habit. The blessings of this habit—for yourself and for others—are incalculable.

## Follow-up Planner

A regular habit of walking with God generates activity beyond just the walking time. It can leave you feeling the need for action—people to call, things to do, places to go. Whether related to business or personal life, ideas for action that come during chats with God are far too important to let slip away. And even the best, most inspired ideas can evaporate quickly if not preserved.

This book is a good example: The idea for writing it came to me during a walk early one morning, complete with the title and a basic outline. It is now nearly ten years later that I'm actually writing it; but the basic ideas are already on paper because I took a few moments to jot down notes after that walk. I will never know whether God planted those ideas in my mind or whether they just sprang from my desire to share an experience that I have found so fulfilling, but at least I did not let the idea disappear.

Major projects are not the only ideas and inspirations that may need follow-through. Prayers for and about others often generate a need to call, send a card to, or visit someone. And praying about our own problems often opens our eyes to good solutions. If you use your walking time to pray, think about your relationship with God, and seek His will in everyday matters, be prepared for ideas. They may not come every day, but they will come—at times in amazing abundance.

You can translate those ideas into actions, but only if you do not let them slip away. It takes only a moment to jot down basic thoughts, but it is time well spent. You can fill in the details later, but if you do not capture their essential elements, some good ideas may be gone forever.

For a couple of dollars you can buy a card file that will hold a year's supply of daily walking cards—a great resource for future reference. Dropping a card into a file box each day only takes a moment, but filing each day's card lets you go back later to recapture ideas you may have forgotten or failed to act upon. Ideas we get from God are worth keeping. Jot them down, drop them in a file box, and be ready to have them spur actions that can make a difference in your life and in the lives of others.

## Walking Data

Most of the space on my walking cards relates to the spiritual part of my daily walks, but there is one section that relates to the physical part.

In any exercise program it is helpful to track your progress. Golfers do this by logging their scores to keep a current "handicap" on the books. Runners often log each run to keep an accurate tally of their overall mileage or to compare their current times with their "personal best." Whatever the sport or exercise, there is usually a tracking system of some kind. Some are simple and others complex, but all are helpful in tracking progress toward goals—formal or informal—that have been established.

Walkers can record several bits of useful information: times; distances; calories burned; and places walked, to name a few. There are special logbooks published for walkers that you can find in bookstores or sporting goods stores. You can also just keep track of the data on the same handy card you carry on each day's walk. If you take the time to jot down ideas or bursts of inspiration you have while walking, it only takes a few seconds more to record significant data about your physical progress.

Distance is the statistic most frequently recorded by walkers, joggers, and runners. Some do this to make sure that each session meets or exceeds a personal minimum standard. Others keep track of distances to provide a growing total of how many miles they have covered in a certain period of time—a month, a year, or even a lifetime. Whatever the purpose, the best way to keep track of distance is to write it down immediately after the walk.

You can keep track of how far you are walking in two good ways. The easiest is to always walk on a measured course such as a track. If you do not have easy access to a measured course, you can create your own by driving along your route and measuring the mileage on your car's odometer. The second method is the pedometer, a device usually worn on the waist that clocks each step and tallies the total distance. You can keep track of your daily distance by either method and record it by simply writing the figure on your walking card. Then if you later want to add up totals or compare your current walking with what you were doing at an earlier time, you will have all the statistical data you need.

Time is the second most frequently kept statistic. Exercise must last at least twenty minutes to produce the aerobic benefit that plays such an important role in cardiovascular health, so many exercisers want to track how they meet or exceed this minimum. You can use any watch to keep track of your time, but most serious exercise walkers use stopwatches. Whether worn on the wrist, hung around the neck, or carried in a pocket, these devices can accurately capture your walking time down to the split second. If you want to keep track of how long you walk each day, be sure to jot down each walk's time. Again, the walking card is a convenient place to make this note.

It is also useful to remember the places where you have walked. If you walk the same route every day, there is little sense in writing it down each time. But if you regularly use different routes, or if you occasionally walk somewhere different, you may find it fun and useful to record those routes. Quick notes about places and distances can remind you of times that were particularly enjoyable, or perhaps of places where you would not want to go walking again. This kind of information is especially useful if you travel to the same places occasionally, serving as a reminder each time of routes you have ferreted out in previous visits. You might even find and record a route so memorable that you will want to recommend it to others. If so, having specific data can be very useful.

*Chapter Five*

# Sharing Your Walk

*"Let us not give up meeting together...but let us encourage one another."*
*—Hebrews 10:25*

God does not intend us to be isolated from one another. It is the nature of humans to seek out others. Look at the number of listings for organizations in your Yellow Pages if you have any doubt. We tend to gravitate toward others with similar interests, and we enjoy sharing whatever we consider most important. So do not be surprised to find yourself wanting to share your walking experience with others once you discover how rewarding it can be.

Walking with others does not mean abandoning the time you spend alone with God. Far from it. Even while preserving these walks as the foundation of your devotional life, you can build upon them by sharing the experience with others. Walking is an easy, relaxed way to build community, and an easy, relaxed atmosphere in which to talk with others about the difference God makes in your own life.

##  Making Connections

Friendship and a sense of community flow naturally when we really get to know one another, and sharing things about ourselves is easier when we are participating in pleasant activities than when we are talking eyeball-to-eyeball. We open up more.

This is why so much business is done on golf courses and over long lunches. It is also why fitness walking is a perfect activity for building relationships as well as good health.

Imagine how well we could get to know others if we had to walk everywhere together, just as Jesus did with His disciples. I do not want to erase all the transportation advances of the past two millennia, but I do envy the way walking drew people together for such long periods of time, breaking down barriers and forcing them to look for common ground. We cannot recapture the dynamics that governed interpersonal relations two thousand years ago, but walking together—even though it is for exercise rather than transportation—still creates an atmosphere in which we can get to know each other better.

When my wife and I were first married, we lived in a large apartment complex built around a lake. (It was really a small pond, but the management got more public relations mileage out of calling it a lake. Whatever it was, it was a wonderful place to walk.) We usually went around that lake at least once each night, talking as we walked hand-in-hand. It was a time for us, as a young married couple, to grow closer by sharing our experiences, feelings, ideas, and dreams. It also established a good habit, and we have continued to enjoy our evening walks through all the years since. The scenery has changed as we have moved from place to place, but the value of the experience is as good as ever.

There is an intimacy in shared activity. It brings people closer together, whether in a workplace, on a tennis court, or along a walking trail. Take a close look at people you see out walking together in your own neighborhood, and you will probably notice that they are talking all the way. Their main purpose may be to get exercise, but they are also getting closer to each other in the process.

For building a stronger relationship with others, it is hard to beat a pleasant, shared activity—particularly one that lends itself to long conversations. Invite someone to go walking with you, and you will invariably get to know that person better. It works with individuals, and it works in groups.

## Getting Closer to Neighbors

People don't seem to know their neighbors as well since front porches started disappearing. In years long past, people could sit in a comfortable rocker on a shady porch and talk to neighbors as they passed by on sidewalks just a few feet away. All of this has changed. Today's suburban homes are typically set far back from the street with decks and patios in the rear instead of front porches. We even build privacy fences to help us stay out of sight. This has its advantages, to be sure, but it does not help us get to know those around us. It is now routine not to know the names of those living even just two houses away, where it was common for people to know everyone in their neighborhoods a couple of generations ago.

Getting to know our neighbors takes effort now. An active neighborhood association or a community pool helps, and children usually bring their parents together with the parents of nearby playmates. Without such natural connections, though, we can go for years without knowing the people on the other side of a fence, and they might be folk we would really enjoy getting to know.

Three women in my neighborhood are up and walking together early almost every morning. Older ladies who just live a couple of houses apart, they hit the streets about seven o'clock for an hour or so of walking and talking. I suspect they have covered every conceivable topic by now—I never see them pass when one of them is not chattering away. They do some serious sharing, and I have no doubt that they have built the kind of lifelong friendships many think disappeared with front porches.

The chances are quite good that there is someone—or several someones—in your neighborhood who would like to walk regularly for exercise. If you want to get to know a neighbor better, ask if he or she would like to join you sometime for one of your daily walks. You might wind up with a regular walking partner, and you may possibly also wind up with a close friend. At the very least, you will break down some of the walls that tend to keep us separated from those around us.

##  Getting Closer to Coworkers

I have worked with some people I really did not want to get to know any better; but there have been others with whom I felt I could become good friends. The workplace does not always lend itself to developing real friendships, however. Schedules and responsibilities often compartmentalize us as well as our tasks, making it difficult to get beyond the surface with the people around us whom we would like to know better. One way to overcome these obstacles is through walking during lunch hours or on exercise breaks.

Thousands of employers have finally recognized the obvious: Healthier employees not only work better but also miss fewer work days. To minimize sick days and medical insurance premiums, more and more companies are encouraging exercise even during work hours. For example, my daughter's first job after college included among its benefits a health club membership, and she was strongly urged to use it.

At some office buildings you will see almost as many gym bags as briefcases carried in each morning.

If your employer allows an exercise break on company time, do not be a martyr and stay chained to your desk. Take advantage of the opportunity to improve your fitness and get better acquainted with some of your coworkers. If exercise time is available, you can bet that others will be walking. Join them, and you will soon find conversation flowing and friendships growing.

If you do not have the option of an exercise break, try walking during your lunch hour. Others working around you may like to do the same, so you are likely to have company once you set this good example. Walking does not require a shower and change of clothes after each session, as long as you do not push for a heart-pounding pace. All it takes is a change of shoes, and off you go. In most cases you can squeeze in a half hour of walking and still have time for lunch before buckling back down to work.

If you are among the growing number of people in home-based businesses, you do not have to feel left out. You have the flexibility to take an exercise break but probably lack the coworkers with whom to walk; however, there are probably others in your neighborhood who are in the same boat. Find another home-based worker and set up a regular walking time. This way you can kill three birds with one stone: a chance to share some good business ideas; get some good exercise; and get better acquainted with a neighbor.

##  Getting Groups Closer

If you have not thought of walking as a group activity, think again. In parks, malls, zoos, and a zillion other places throughout America, people get together every day to walk for exercise. There is usually some other reason for their coming together, but walking is the activity that binds them. One of the most common reasons for forming or joining a walking group is weight loss. Most diet programs—*any* that are worth their salt—include exercise as a primary component. Simply cutting calories and fat is not enough. Taking weight off and *keeping* it off requires a lifestyle change, and this includes a regular habit of exercise. Not surprisingly, many walking groups spin off from weight-loss programs.

Senior citizens are big on group walking, too. Without the structured schedules dictated by jobs, seniors often have to look for good reasons to get together with others. Walking is a natural because it is a fitness exercise most can do as long as they live. Shopping malls across America are now making a point of attracting seniors who like to walk together, even opening early to let them in before the shopping hordes descend. They come early, walk together, and then wind up spending some time—and money—enjoying each others' company over breakfast in the mall's food court. "Mall walkers" coast to coast are enjoying this wonderful combination of social and fitness activity.

Many churches are forming walking groups, too. The days are past when most church activities seemed to add calories instead of burning them up. Ice cream socials and family night dinners have not disappeared, but family life centers—complete with facilities and programs to help members stay physically healthy—have become central parts of many churches. If walking with a group might keep you at it better than walking alone, check to see if your church has a fitness walking group. If not, maybe it has been waiting for you to start one.

##  Sharing Common Interests

Whenever we walk with others, whether with coworkers and neighbors or with church or community groups, we have an opportunity to share common interests. This is an increasingly rare privilege. As technological and societal changes have altered America's living patterns, it is easier than ever for us to become isolated. This is not the way we are created to live. We are not like ants and bees, to just keep plugging away as anonymous drones. We function better when we celebrate our individuality by interacting with others in healthy and natural ways.

Our interests bring us together, as any parent can confirm. When my daughter was five years old, we knew the parents of every five-year-old for blocks around. Golfers seek out other golfers. Quilters seek out other quilters. We may not always have as much time as we would really like to spend on our interests, but we gravitate to others who share them.

Not surprisingly, Christians gravitate toward other Christians. When the church becomes the focus for a family's activities, it usually leads to close friendships with others in the same congregation. Our common belief in and devotion to God is perhaps our ultimate shared interest. Wanting to spend time with each other in settings other than a sanctuary or Sunday school classroom is a natural result. What better way than to walk together, sharing and growing in faith as well as in friendship?

## Walking Witness

Few things strike fear in the hearts of some Christians as much as the prospect of witnessing to others. Being called on to pray out loud in Sunday School is enough of a strain, let alone taking on the task of leading someone to the Lord. At the theoretical level we may want to reach out, but when the need is right in front of us, fear and trembling of biblical proportions can quickly set in. This is not true for all, of course. Some Christians jump into witnessing as though they were born—or born again—for the task.

*"Go...to your friends and tell them how much the Lord has done for you."*
*—Mark 5:19 (NRSV)*

But for many the charge to "go and make disciples of all nations" (Matt. 28:19) is easier to deal with in the abstract than up close and personal. That is probably why some churches stress international missions more than the pressing needs just outside their sanctuary doors. God's love is not just for a favored few, however; it is for everyone. Some people close to us will not learn the good news of Christ if we do not tell them.

We have something to share, and everyone needs the message of salvation even if they do not realize it. Whether physical, emotional, or even economic, every kind of suffering can be relieved, and we know the secret of the ultimate source for assurance and peace. Jesus said, "Come to me, all you who are weary and burdened, and I will give you rest" (Matt. 11:28). He did not say "all you who belong to a particular church, are a particular color, live in a particular neighborhood, or are in a particular economic bracket." He simply said "Come to Me, *all* ..." Having known the peace and comfort of God's love, how can we not jump at the chance to share with others?

You have probably had someone knock on your door and ask if you are saved. Some churches and denominations use a door-to-door approach to witnessing, ready to explain the plan of salvation to any who will listen. This is effective in some cases, but is not often the best approach to evangelism.

The dictionary defines a *witness* as "someone who has knowledge of something." This brings it to a personal level, which is precisely where witnessing should be. Through our own relationship with God, we have something personal to share. Witnessing is as simple as telling someone else of our own feelings and experiences, and how God's grace has touched our lives.

Opportunities for effective witnessing abound. Along with success, progress, and comfort, our society is laced with insecurity, stumbling, and pain. We need look no further than the soaring use of drugs and alcohol to realize that all is not well; and we are just kidding ourselves if we think the solution lies in just locking up the symptoms. We will never lick the problems that plague today's society until we deal with the underlying causes. Behind each human problem is a living, breathing person who needs help—and one of those in need may be as close as the apartment or house next door.

The most effective witnessing most people can do is *targeted witnessing*—recognizing that a specific person needs help and working with this person's individual needs. We cannot all lead evangelistic crusades like Billy Graham or influence millions through example like Jimmy Carter, but we can all quietly and calmly lead others to know our Savior. Making it personal makes it effective. We simply need to do what Jesus said two thousand years ago: "Go … and tell how much the Lord has done for you" (Mark 5:19).

If you want to create an atmosphere for witnessing that is easy and not at all intimidating, try walking with the person about whom you are concerned. It can begin as a fitness effort, but the regular time you spend so closely together sets a stage for conversation. This is a stepping-off point for talking openly about what God has meant, and continues to mean, in your own life.

*"Come to me, all you who are weary and burdened, and I will give you rest. Take my yoke upon you and learn from me, for I am gentle and humble in heart, and you will find rest for your souls."*
*—Matthew 11:28–29*

 ## Helping with a Problem

Witnessing to another person does not mean whipping out a five-step plan of salvation and launching into a hard sell. In fact, this is one of the quickest ways to turn most people off. When the situation is right for walking someone through a prepared list of Bible verses and witnessing points, go for it. In most cases, though, the quickest way to get through to others is to help them understand that a relationship with God is the answer to their problems.

These are words of comfort for anyone who is hurting—words of gentleness, acceptance, and forgiveness, direct from Jesus for all people. Time has not eroded their impact, and people are hungry for their reassurance—perhaps more than ever before.

Most people tend to suffer in silence rather than open up to others. This is not anything new, but it means that millions are hurting, some of them right around us. Marriages, children, relationships, jobs, the financial tightrope—the list of worries is virtually endless, and the burden can get awfully heavy. Yet there is a loving God who wants to help with personal burdens, take them to Himself, and give rest to our souls. This is the message that those who are suffering truly need to hear.

Sometimes it is hard to offer help to someone with a personal problem, even if we know about it. A kind word can help, of course, as can a prayer that you offer on their behalf. Personal contact, though, can be very meaningful. Most hurting people need someone to talk with, particularly if this someone has personal knowledge of something that the person needs.

If you do not feel comfortable launching into a discussion of a problem you know a friend is having, why not invite this person to join you for walking? You do not have to mention the problem. Just walk together, and the odds are that a couple of good, long walks will turn the conversation to whatever the burden might be. Walking generates honest communication, a foundation for the kind of trust that brings out a willingness to share even our deepest concerns.

And most people just want someone to listen. You can be that good listener while walking, and you can also help introduce a troubled friend to someone else who is a good listener: *God*. Walking together, talking together, and praying together combine to create a powerful means to witness. It is not intimidating, just life-changing.

## Inviting Someone to Church

When I was seven or eight years old, a regular event during my Sunday School time was sharing how many contacts we had made during the previous week. The idea was to have people—even young children—invite their friends to church and tally up the total numbers each week. Looking back, I fear it was more a numbers game than effective outreach. My friends and I would pull numbers out of the air, figuring that if we had mentioned the word "church" to someone during the preceding week, this should count.

Inviting a friend to church is easy. All we have to do is open our mouths and do it. The trick is to do it in such a way that the person wants to take us up on the invitation and actually show up. Walking together can set the stage for this.

If you have a friend with no church, or even one who belongs to a church but rarely darkens its doors, the slow, leisurely conversation of long walks can let this subject emerge naturally. Simply by talking about your own life and activities you are likely to venture into tales of what happened in Sunday School, at a family-night fellowship, at choir practice, or at some other church activity. It is a natural way to lay out an important part of your life for your friends to see. Then it is just a short step to ask them to join you.

Inviting someone to church does not mean just suggesting they show up at a Sunday morning worship service, either. Think of how your friend might fit in some other activity of your church, perhaps even one that does not occur on Sundays. I have friends whose entire families are deeply involved in church activities, and who are truly committed Christians, but who would never have stepped through the door if their children had not attended a church-sponsored preschool or "Mother's Day Out" program.

There is nothing strained or artificial about inviting a fellow walker to church. It is a natural outgrowth of being together in the close communion that walking creates, and it has the potential for that other person to find an even more meaningful kind of communion. For that person, walking with a friend can be the first step toward walking with God.

##  Candid Talk about Salvation

When you start walking with someone who is not a committed Christian, that person may ask you about your own faith. Your walking partner may sense something in your life that is missing from her own, or her questions may spring simply from curiosity about something that is obviously important to you. You may be more than ready to answer these questions, but it can be disconcerting when you are not.

Talking about Christ to non-Christians does not require years of Bible study. Anyone who enjoys a close relationship with God has firsthand experience of how God reveals Himself. When we tell of our own experiences with God and share what has happened in our own lives, we are witnessing. We may not be quoting Scripture or following a prescribed set of steps, but we are telling what Christ has meant specifically to us. The next logical step is to point out that God's light and grace is freely available to everyone.

If you want to review the basics of the Christian message, it is easy to do. There are enough books about the essential truths of salvation to fill a library. Each pastor, denomination, and theologian may place more or less emphasis on some of the points, but most Christians will agree on some basic tenets of God's miraculous plan. Here are some worthy of jotting down on your walking cards:

> *"I am the light of the world. Whoever follows me will never walk in darkness, but will have the light of life."*
> *—John 8:12*

None of us is perfect. We are all sinners.
*"For all have sinned and fall short of the glory of God" (Rom. 3:23).*

Sin ultimately separates us from God forever.
*"For the wages of sin is death" (Rom. 6:23).*

God is merciful and offers an alternative.
*"The Lord…is patient with you, not wanting anyone to perish, but everyone to come to repentance" (2 Peter 3:9).*

We must repent of our sins.
*"Repent, then, and turn to God, so that your sins may be wiped out" (Acts 3:19).*

Jesus experienced death so we would not have to.
*"God demonstrates His own love for us in this: While we were still sinners, Christ died for us" (Rom. 5:8).*

We must believe that what Jesus did for us was real.
*"If you confess with your mouth, 'Jesus is Lord' and believe in your heart that God raised him from the dead, you will be saved" (Rom. 10:9).*

Salvation is free. We do not have to earn it. We only have to accept God's miraculous gift.
*"For it is by grace you have been saved, through faith—and this not from yourselves, it is the gift of God" (Eph. 2:8).*

God's love is overwhelming, and we can enjoy a personal relationship with Him throughout eternity.

*"For God so loved the world that he gave his one and only Son, that whoever believes in him shall not perish but have eternal life" (John 3:16).*

An old hymn dear to many hearts begins: "We've a story to tell to the nations." While this is a hymn about missions, not everyone is called to be a career missionary, and "the nations" does not mean just faraway places. Each of us has a story to tell, a story both biblical and personal. For the biblical part, we can jot down Scripture references on a card to use as memory joggers when we walk with friends who ask us about our faith. For the personal part, we need merely speak from the heart, telling what God has done for us and how our lives have been changed by the relationship we share.

 ## Nurturing Each Other

Witnessing does not mean just telling the unsaved about Christ. We also are called to show Christian love to each other. Jesus said, "My command is this: Love each other as I have loved you" (John 15:12). Throughout the New Testament, over and over again, we are reminded of our obligations to each other.

*"Carry each other's burdens, and in this way you will fulfill the law of Christ" (Gal. 6:2).*

*"Be kind and compassionate to one another, forgiving each other, just as in Christ God forgave you" (Eph. 4:32).*

*"Agree with each other in the Lord" (Phil. 4:2).*

*"Bear with each other and forgive whatever grievances you may have against one another. Forgive as the Lord forgave you" (Col. 3:13).*

*"Therefore encourage each other with these words" (1 Thess. 4:18).*

*"Live in peace with each other" (1 Thess. 5:13).*

*"Be kind to each other and to everyone else" (1 Thess. 5:15).*

*"Above all, love each other deeply, because love covers over a multitude of sins" (1 Peter 4:8).*

Nurturing love should come so naturally to Christians that caring for other believers is second nature—certainly as urgent a priority as reaching out to the unsaved. This is not always the case, however. Sometimes we overlook the needs of those closest to us while focusing on those beyond.

I once had a neighbor who was active in organizations throughout the community, spending hours each day working on programs aimed at helping children. Unfortunately, she spent so much time in meetings that her own children virtually became latchkey kids. When I last saw her, she was leading a teen drug organization, because her own children had become hooked on drugs. I have wondered whether these problems could have been avoided if she had paid as much attention to the home front as she did to the world beyond. Reaching out is a charge we have been given as Christians, and it is a charge we must keep; but we cannot afford to neglect our own family of faith in the process.

*"The prayer of a righteous man is powerful and effective."*

*—James 5:16*

One of the best ways we can care for each other, as the Bible reminds us, is to pray for each other.

Wednesday night prayer meetings are among the sweet memories of my childhood. A faithful few gathered at our church in the middle of the week, sang a hymn or two, heard a few words from the pastor, and then did lots of praying. Some of the prayers were spoken aloud, but most of the time we prayed silently, each person in the small group mentioning persons who needed our prayers. This was my introduction to intercessory prayer, and it taught me the power in this calm, quiet ministry.

Prayer does not require kneeling. It does not require being still. It does not even require being alone in the way that I enjoy using solitary walking for conversations with God. Prayer can also occur while walking in groups, with exercise partners becoming prayer partners, too.

The same principles for solitary walking with God can work when walking with a Christian friend or with several friends. Together you can use walking cards to focus on daily jewels of biblical guidance. Together you can share your thoughts on how a focus thought applies to your own lives. Together you can even sing a hymn or praise song as you walk along. Then together you can pray—aloud or silently—about shared concerns you have for yourselves and for others whose burdens you have taken into your hearts. Jesus Himself has told us how powerful joining together for prayer can be: "I tell you that if two of you on earth agree about anything you ask for, it will be done for you by my Father in heaven" (Matt. 18:19).

Our faith may be individual and our relationship with God may be very personal, but we are called to fellowship with each other, to care for each other, to pray for each other. Jesus said, "Where two or three come together in my name, there am I with them" (Matt. 18:20). He was with His disciples on the dusty roads of Galilee, and He is with us when we join with others to combine exercise and reflection as we walk with God.

*Chapter Six*

# Walking for Health and Weight

*"This will bring health to your body and nourishment to your bones."*
*—Proverbs 3:8*

Ask any group of fitness walkers why they exercise, and two words crop up every time: *health* and *weight*. Both are sound reasons to make walking a habit. In its *Healthy People 2000* report, the US Department of Health and Human Services placed physical activity and fitness at the top of eight categories that affect Americans' health, with nutrition next in line. Unfortunately millions have not seen the light and continue moving steadily toward potential disaster simply by ignoring what is now common knowledge: inactivity kills, but sensible exercise leads to good health.

A study by the Centers for Disease Control found that inactive people have twice the risk of heart disease as those who stay active. Another study covering 55,000 men in the greater New York area concluded that men are almost four times as likely to die from a heart attack if they are inactive. And the Institute of Aerobics Research in Dallas conducted the largest study ever done on fitness and the risk of dying, finding that even moderate levels of exercise greatly reduce the risks of death. Inactivity increases the risk of heart disease as much as smoking a pack of cigarettes every day, and heart disease claims a half-million American lives each year. This should be enough to get anyone's attention!

The connection between exercise and a healthy heart is well known, but this is just the beginning of a very long list. Exercise also has positive effects on many other diseases and conditions, from cancer to constipation. Walking can help prevent and manage high blood pressure, Type II diabetes, osteoporosis, obesity, and mental health problems. It has been associated with lower rates of stroke, colon cancer, and orthopedic problems. It strengthens bones, helps ensure safe pregnancies, and is a proven path to better health in many other ways. No wonder so many doctors now recommend walking.

On the average, people who are physically active outlive those who are not—and good health lets them *enjoy* those years more fully as well. Regular walking can lower a person's biological age, sometimes as much as ten to twenty years below chronological age. Just as important, it can improve the quality of life each day.

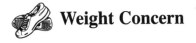 ## Weight Concern

Quality of life depends on many factors, and one of the most pervasive is weight. Too much weight can limit everything from self-image to lifespan, and the desire to lose weight has motivated millions of people to walk. Polls show that four out of five American adults think they are overweight, and many are right. Some dieters chase the slim body image only because Hollywood and advertisers portray this as the ideal. But truly overweight persons face potential consequences that are much more serious than an out-of-fashion image.

About 20 percent of Americans are seriously fat, though we usually choose a more delicate term—*obese*—for those who weigh at least 30 percent more than their ideal body weight. Whatever the word, more than forty million Americans fit this definition. Along with these extra pounds they carry an increased risk of diabetes, high blood pressure, high cholesterol, heart disease, and other chronic illnesses.

This is far more than an image problem. It is a serious health concern for one in every five Americans, and for many it is literally a matter of life and death. A fifty-year-old person who is 40 percent overweight can expect to live ten years less than one at the ideal weight. Fortunately this problem is not beyond our control. Extra pounds can subtract years from life expectancy, but subtracting the extra pounds can add this life expectancy right back.

In study after study, formerly overweight people have been pronounced healthier than ever. For example, an American Dietetic Association study found that overweight people who lost 10 to 20 percent of their body weight and kept it off for three years had significantly lower risks of high blood pressure, diabetes, and heart disease than they had before.

As the health-related impacts of excess weight have become better understood in recent years, dieting has been approached from every conceivable angle. From popcorn to pineapples and from rice to running, various foods and fads have been heralded as the ultimate weapons in the battle of the bulge. But quick fixes rarely yield long-term results. Abandoned diet books and exercise equipment bear silent testimony to the futility of methods that are long on promise but short on results. Abandoned hopes abound, too, with millions of disillusioned dieters believing they are doomed to carry extra weight for the rest of their lives. They could not be more wrong.

Faddish weight-loss methods may not live up to expectations, but there *is* a method with proven success. It is not quick, and it is not always easy, but it works. Best of all, its results are lasting—not just temporary losses that spring right back as soon as some extraordinary regimen ends. This method most of us learned in our seventh-grade health classes, and it has kept people healthy for thousands of years: *sensible diet combined with moderate exercise.*

This is not an exotic approach requiring special foods, weekly meetings, or high program costs. It just requires some sensible changes in daily routines and eating habits. By following a few steps, you can achieve what millions dream of: losing weight and keeping it off.

If weight loss is one of your motivations for starting to exercise, follow this time-tested route instead of glittery but less effective fads. The following pages outline a ten-step process for combining sensible diet with comfortable fitness walking. Use these steps to personalize a program of exercise and diet, and you will be amazed at the results. It takes a little commitment and energy, but it works. Having lost 50 pounds myself using these principles, I am living proof!

## Charting a Weight-Loss Course

Mapping out a weight-loss program begins in the same way as mapping out a trip: know where you are and decide where you want to end up. Use the following ten steps to tailor a plan of diet and exercise to your specific needs. Break all the rules you learned in school about not writing in books. Fill in the blanks, and by the end of this chapter you will have your own personal road map to health.

## Step 1: *Find Your Current Weight*

The first step is easy. Simply find a good set of scales and weigh yourself. It does not really matter what time of day you choose to weigh, but always weigh at roughly the same time of day so you will have valid comparisons. Because we weigh the least just after waking up, many physiologists recommend weighing in the morning. *Consistency* is the key: Weighing at about the same time of day each time is the only way to accurately track your progress.

*Enter your current weight:* _____

## Step 2: *Determine Your Goal Weight*

Once you know where you are, you need to decide on your specific goal. A general goal of losing weight or getting into those too-tight slacks in the closet is not enough. For optimum health goals, we should know our ideal weight. Health professionals have developed charts that give us this information based on our individual height, sex, age, muscle mass, and other factors. These charts vary slightly depending on source, but are usually in the same range. The body-mass index (BMI) chart will help you determine an appropriate target weight.

But keep in mind that self-evaluation calls for honesty, and this is sometimes difficult to summon where weight is concerned. Deceiving ourselves about body type, bone size, or other factors may make us feel better, but it does not help us establish realistic goals. When I weighed 215 pounds as a fifteen-year-old, my mother tried to excuse it by saying I had "big bones." Actually, my bones were medium; they were just covered with so much fat that no one could tell!

An important factor to remember in determining weight goals is the amount of muscle you have. When you lose weight you want to lose *fat*, not muscle. Some very large people (NFL linemen for example) have a very low percentage of body fat and are therefore considered lean and not overweight. Aim to take off pounds by decreasing body fat. Setting your goals according to your BMI will help in this area.

Look down the left column to find your height. Follow that line to the weight nearest your own. Look to the top or middle of the column to find your BMI.

*Record your BMI here:* _____

According to the World Health Organization, overweight is classified as a BMI of 25 to 29.9 for women and men ages 19-69. Obesity is a BMI over 30, and severe obesity is over 40. If you are in the overweight or obese range, select a goal weight that puts you in a healthy BMI range.

# Body Mass Index

| BMI | 19 | 20 | 21 | 22 | 23 | 24 | 25 | 26 | 27 | 28 | 29 | 30 | 35 | 40 |
|-----|----|----|----|----|----|----|----|----|----|----|----|----|----|----|
| 4-10 | 90.7 | 95.5 | 100.3 | 105.0 | 109.8 | 114.6 | 119.4 | 124.1 | 128.9 | 128.9 | 138.5 | 143.2 | 167.1 | 191.0 |
| 4-11 | 93.9 | 98.8 | 103.8 | 108.7 | 113.6 | 118.6 | 123.5 | 128.5 | 133.4 | 133.4 | 143.3 | 148.2 | 172.9 | 197.6 |
| 5-0 | 97.1 | 102.2 | 107.3 | 112.4 | 117.5 | 122.6 | 127.7 | 132.9 | 138.0 | 138.0 | 148.2 | 155.3 | 178.8 | 204.4 |
| 5-1 | 100.3 | 105.6 | 110.9 | 116.2 | 121.5 | 126.8 | 132.0 | 137.3 | 142.6 | 142.6 | 153.2 | 158.4 | 184.8 | 211.3 |
| 5-2 | 103.7 | 109.1 | 114.6 | 120.0 | 125.5 | 130.9 | 136.4 | 141.9 | 147.3 | 147.3 | 158.2 | 163.7 | 191.0 | 218.2 |
| 5-3 | 107.0 | 112.7 | 118.3 | 123.9 | 129.6 | 135.2 | 140.8 | 146.5 | 152.1 | 152.1 | 163.4 | 169.0 | 197.2 | 225.3 |
| 5-4 | 110.5 | 116.3 | 122.1 | 127.9 | 133.7 | 139.5 | 145.3 | 151.2 | 157.0 | 157.0 | 168.3 | 174.4 | 203.5 | 232.5 |
| 5-5 | 113.9 | 119.9 | 125.9 | 131.9 | 137.9 | 143.9 | 149.9 | 155.9 | 161.9 | 161.9 | 173.9 | 179.9 | 209.9 | 239.9 |
| 5-6 | 117.5 | 123.7 | 129.8 | 136.0 | 142.2 | 148.4 | 154.6 | 160.8 | 166.9 | 166.9 | 179.3 | 185.2 | 216.4 | 247.3 |
| 5-7 | 121.1 | 127.4 | 133.8 | 140.2 | 146.5 | 152.9 | 159.3 | 165.7 | 172.0 | 172.0 | 184.8 | 191.1 | 223.0 | 254.9 |
| 5-8 | 124.7 | 131.3 | 137.8 | 144.4 | 151.0 | 157.5 | 164.1 | 170.6 | 177.2 | 177.2 | 190.3 | 196.9 | 230.2 | 262.5 |
| 5-9 | 128.4 | 135.2 | 141.9 | 148.7 | 155.4 | 162.2 | 168.9 | 175.7 | 182.5 | 182.5 | 196.0 | 202.7 | 236.5 | 270.3 |
| 5-10 | 132.1 | 139.1 | 146.1 | 153.0 | 160.0 | 166.9 | 173.9 | 180.8 | 187.8 | 187.8 | 201.7 | 208.6 | 249.4 | 278.2 |
| 5-11 | 135.9 | 143.1 | 150.3 | 157.4 | 164.6 | 171.7 | 178.9 | 186.0 | 193.2 | 193.2 | 207.5 | 214.6 | 250.4 | 286.2 |
| 6-0 | 139.8 | 147.2 | 154.5 | 161.9 | 169.2 | 176.6 | 183.9 | 191.3 | 198.7 | 198.7 | 213.4 | 220.7 | 257.5 | 294.3 |
| 6-1 | 143.7 | 151.3 | 158.8 | 166.4 | 174.0 | 181.5 | 189.1 | 196.7 | 204.2 | 204.2 | 219.3 | 226.9 | 264.7 | 302.5 |
| 6-2 | 147.7 | 155.4 | 163.2 | 171.0 | 178.8 | 186.5 | 194.3 | 202.1 | 209.9 | 209.9 | 225.4 | 233.2 | 272.0 | 310.9 |
| 6-3 | 151.7 | 159.7 | 167.6 | 175.6 | 183.6 | 191.6 | 199.6 | 207.6 | 215.6 | 215.6 | 231.5 | 239.5 | 279.4 | 319.4 |
| 6-4 | 155.8 | 164.0 | 172.2 | 180.4 | 188.6 | 196.8 | 205.0 | 213.2 | 221.4 | 221.4 | 237.7 | 245.9 | 286.9 | 327.9 |

**CHART NO. 1: BMI CHART**

Note: A BMI from 20 to 24.9 is desirable for most young and middle-aged adults. For adults over 55, a BMI up to 29 may be considered normal if they are in very good health.

*Record your goal weight here:* _____

<u>Step 3:</u> *Decide How Much Weight You Need to Lose*

$$\underline{\hspace{3cm}} \quad - \quad \underline{\hspace{3cm}} \quad = \quad \underline{\hspace{3cm}}$$
*(current weight)*     *(goal weight)*   *(pounds to lose)*

<u>Step 4:</u> *Find the Calorie Deficit You Need*

Reduced to its simplest form, losing weight is a matter of spending more calories than you take in. When you overspend by 3,500 calories, you lose a pound. To lose more pounds, just multiply your weight loss goal by 3,500 and you will know the total number of calories you must overspend.

$$\underline{\hspace{3cm}} \quad \text{x} \quad \underline{\hspace{1.5cm}3,500\hspace{1.5cm}} \quad = \quad \underline{\hspace{2.5cm}}$$
*(pounds to lose)*    *(calories per pound)*    *(calorie deficit)*

 **Calories DO Count!**

A popular myth holds that calories no longer count. This is nonsense. Despite theories to the contrary, calories *do* count, and we have to count them if we are serious about weight control.

    Calories are not mystical elements that sneak into our bodies and suddenly explode into fat. They are simply a method for measuring the fuel our bodies receive and the energy we use in burning it up. Counting calories is like watching the gas gauge on a car. We must make sure we always have enough without making the tank overflow every time we stop for a refill.

    A calorie is simply the unit by which we measure the energy value of our food. Scientifically, it is a precise measure of heat—the amount needed to raise the temperature of one milliliter of water one degree centigrade. Since our bodies produce heat as we expend energy (something readily apparent to anyone who has ever worked up a sweat), we can measure the heat as a number of calories burned. With food providing fuel for the body, we can also compute the number of burnable calories each type and amount of food contains.

    If we do not burn up all the calories we take in, they have to be stored somewhere —and this is where fat comes from. The body tucks away the extra fuel as fat cells, distributing them from head to toe. As long as it gets more calories than it burns up, the body will keep storing up fat. When the body takes in fewer calories than it needs, it turns to the fuel it has stored up—fat—and burns whatever it needs.

You can look at your calorie count in the same way you might look at a bank account. Every mouthful of food is a deposit, and every activity that requires energy —even just breathing—is a withdrawal. If we deposit more than we withdraw, the surplus grows larger and larger—most visibly at our waist and hips. But if we have start withdrawing more than we deposit, the "bottom line" will drop rapidly.

Each pound of body weight equals 3,500 calories. If you spend 3,500 more calories than you deposit, you lose a pound. If you take in 3,500 more than you expend, you gain a pound. Thus we see that calories do count and how counting calories allows you to design a weight-loss program in precise and measurable terms.

##  Why Include Exercise?

Since weight loss results from burning more calories than you take in, there are two ways to lose weight. You can either reduce the input (the number of calories you consume), or you can increase the output (the number of calories you burn up). For best results, do both.

Diet alone is not the best long-term solution. It might produce a quick loss, but quick weight losses from fad diets are usually temporary, with weight rebounding to where it was before—and often shooting even higher. Our bodies will surrender some pounds when starved or abused, but they grab them back when given half a chance.

"Yo-yo dieting" can become a dangerous lifetime pattern. According to the National Center for Dietetics, chronic dieting, under-eating, and meal skipping— often the key ingredients of crash diets—contribute to a sluggish metabolism. This slowdown in metabolism makes it increasingly hard to lose weight, and each new diet becomes more difficult than the one before. Also, without exercise, about one-third of a person's weight loss is from lean tissue instead of fat. This can lead to weakness and muscle deterioration. When you exercise you lose more of what you really want to lose—the fat.

Walking is so effective at burning calories that it can actually produce weight loss with no dieting at all. Walking a mile at a very moderate pace for fifteen minutes burns up about one hundred calories. Compare this with the fifteen to twenty calories you burn by watching television for the same length of time, and you can see that substituting a half-hour walk for one daily soap opera or sitcom can burn up an extra 160 to 170 calories. Over about three weeks, this practice can produce a one-pound weight loss as long as your diet stays stable. Combine the walking with sensible eating, though, and the weight goes away more quickly, as do health risks.

To have an even more effective exercise regimen, supplement your walking with strength training. The more muscle you build, the more calories you burn, even at rest. Though muscle weighs more than fat, it is metabolically more active. Adding two pounds of muscle weight will burn 125–150 extra calories a day. And the leaner you are, the healthier you are. Some simple exercises you can use after your walk are included in chapter 11.

The facts about exercise are clear, but many of us are just not willing to act on them. More than two-thirds of the sedentary people surveyed by the President's Council on Physical Fitness and Sports said they would *like* to exercise more but simply cannot find the time. More accurately, they do not *take* the time. They did report finding time for couch-potato activities such as watching television.

Walking works for two reasons: First, it burns calories efficiently—at about the same rate per mile as jogging. A slower pace does not mean fewer benefits. It just means taking a bit longer to obtain them. Second, people will actually do it. The physical effort of walking is acceptable to millions who would reject more strenuous sports such as jogging or aerobics. This is why the dropout rate is lower for walking than for any other form of exercise—and no exercise can be effective if people are unwilling to do it.

Losing weight is easiest when we know precisely how many calories are going in and out of our bodies. The "going in" part is not too difficult. Lots of books are available that show the calorie content of various foods. Figuring out how many calories we burn up, however, is something we must calculate for ourselves.

The number of calories you burn in an average day depends on your body weight, activity level, and metabolism. Some people seem able to eat anything they want and never gain a pound (a condition with which I am not blessed), while others who weigh about the same can seem to gain a pound just by looking at food. This is a result one's metabolism, the rate at which the body converts calories into energy.

The basic metabolism—called *basal metabolism*—varies somewhat from person to person, but it usually amounts to about ten calories per day for each pound of body weight. This is the number of calories you will burn just by staying alive and breathing, but additional calories are burned by every activity of living.

While crash dieting can lead to a sluggish metabolism, combining walking with sensible dieting can actually speed up your metabolism. The body burns calories at a higher rate during exercise, and it keeps burning them at a higher rate for several hours afterward. Instead of burning the usual one-calorie-per-minute while sedentary, the body's post-exercise rate can be increased by two or three times this figure. Studies have shown that this increase can continue for up to six hours after an exercise session, depending on the length and intensity of the activity.

To get an accurate reading of how many calories you burn in a day, you must add your basal metabolism to the calories you burn in your daily activities.

## Step 5: *Determine Your Daily Metabolism*

Basic metabolism varies from person to person. A good rule of thumb is to base it on ten calories per day for each pound you weigh for women and eleven calories per day for men.

    <u>10 (or 11)</u>   x  _____  =  _____

     *(calories)*    *(current weight)*   *(basic daily metabolism)*

## Step 6: *Determine How Many Activity Calories You Burn*

Add the calories you burn in activities to your basic metabolism calories, and you will have a fairly accurate estimate how many calories you actually use each day.

    The Institute for Aerobic Research's *Walking Handbook* suggests calculating those additional calories as a percentage of the basic calories, with your personal percentage depending on how active you are. On a scale with 30 percent representing a sedentary lifestyle and 80 percent representing an extremely active lifestyle, select a percentage that reflects how active you are. Consider such factors as whether you exercise regularly, whether you have active hobbies such as gardening or hiking, and how much physical exertion your daily work requires.

     30% = Sedentary
     50% = Moderately Active
     80% = Extremely Active

*Estimate your activity level as a percentage between 30% and 80%:* _____

    _____   +   _____   =   _____

   *(basic metabolism*    *(activity percentage*   *(activity calories)*
   *calories—from step 5)*   *—from chart above)*

## <u>Step 7</u>: *Determine How Many Total Calories You Burn Daily:*

Now add your basic metabolism calories and your activity calories to see how many calories you are burning up each day at your present activity level.

_____ + _____ = _____

*(basic metabolism*      *(activity calories*      *(total calories*
*calories—from step 5)*      *—from step 6)*      *burned)*

## <u>Step 8:</u> *Determine the Weekly Calorie Deficit You Need:*

Losing a pound requires burning 3,500 more calories than you take in, so it is a simple matter of deposits and withdrawals. Checking your food intake with any good calorie counter book can give you a feel for your current daily deposits, and the chart in Step 7 gives a picture of your daily withdrawals. With this information, deciding how quickly you want to reach your weight goal is a matter of deciding how many fewer calories you will take in each day.

Divide your daily calorie deficit into the total calorie deficit needed to reach your goal (Step 4), and you can see how long it will take. Consuming five hundred fewer calories than you burn each day, for example, should result in a one-pound weight loss in one week. If your goal (from Step 2) is to lose ten pounds, you must burn 35,000 more calories than you consume, so it would take ten weeks to reach your goal.

Approaching weight loss with more enthusiasm than realism has been the downfall of many a diet. Deciding to lose five pounds a week, for example, simply is not realistic for most people. This would require consuming 17,500 fewer calories than you burn, and this would allow only 250 calories per day for a moderately active, 150-pound person. No one can live very long on such a starvation diet. Unrealistic goals set us up for failure—diets abandoned either because the weight loss did not come as quickly as expected or because the starvation was simply too tough to take.

Most diet and exercise specialists now say that one pound per week is about the ideal rate for weight loss. This rate may be slower than in some crash diet pro-grams, but it will not damage the body. Taking in fewer than 1,200 calories a day deprives the body of essential nutrients, causing the body to break down its lean body tissue—not fat—for the blood sugar it must have. This is simply not healthy. Another good reason for going more slowly is that keeping weight off requires changing basic habits, and this only occurs when the diet is reasonable, the exercise is enjoyable, and we are willing to sustain the healthier lifestyle long after reaching our ideal weight.

How far are you willing to cut your daily calorie intake? By choosing foods wisely, you may not have to cut too much. One gram of fat, for example, equals nine calories. But one gram of protein or carbohydrate equals only four calories.

How many extra calories are you really willing to burn through exercise? Are you willing to add muscle mass that will burn calories at rest? Be honest in the estimate you use for figuring the pace you are willing to keep. You may need to try this formula several times to find a realistic goal.

$$\underline{\hspace{2cm}} - \underline{\hspace{2cm}} = \quad = \quad \underline{\hspace{2cm}}$$

<table>
<tr><td>(total calorie<br>deficit—step 4)</td><td>(weeks to<br>reach goal)</td><td>=</td><td>(weekly calorie deficit)</td></tr>
</table>

 ## Balancing Diet and Exercise

You can produce the calorie deficit needed to lose weight in either of two ways: cut the calorie intake, or raise the rate at which you burn them. Either way will work on its own, but it is best to combine the two. Exercise increases metabolism so that calories burn faster during the activity and for up to six hours afterward. Combine the higher rate of burning calories with taking in fewer of them and you have a sensible weight loss program.

For burning calories and fat, walking is among the best of all exercises. Other sports such as tennis and racquetball are more intense but involve short bursts of energy that burn more carbohydrates than fat. It is the fat that you want to lose and the moderate, constant movement of walking burns more fat than carbohydrates. Also, unlike more strenuous sports, walking will not dramatically increase your post-exercise appetite.

To lose weight and reduce your percentage of body fat, the American College of Sports Medicine recommends exercising three to five times per week and burning at least three hundred calories in each session. For most people, walking about three miles at a moderate pace will meet this goal. This three-hundred-calories-per-session measuring stick is important, as studies have shown that burning *fewer* than three hundred calories lowers the effect of exercise on weight loss dramatically.

Fortunately, you do not need to burn those three hundred calories per session in high stress exercise. It can be done by running twenty to thirty minutes or by walking forty to sixty minutes. Contrary to popular belief, walking and running burn approximately the same number of calories per mile. You will burn off about the same calories whether walking a mile in fifteen minutes or jogging it in 8.5 minutes. The primary differences are the time it takes and the toll it takes on your body's load-bearing joints.

Since walking for weight loss is a matter of distance rather than speed, you can walk off more weight by simply walking farther rather than faster. A walking pace of about 3.3 to 3.7 miles per hour rate gets the job done quite nicely and is a comfortable "middle gear" for most people. Comfort is important, too: Too many enthusiastic new exercisers start out by overdoing a good thing. Hundreds of overweight people each year die or suffer serious injury by starting to exercise at levels that overtax their physical capabilities. Walking does not present this problem, since its benefits accrue from simply going farther, not faster.

To use walking to help create a calorie deficit and lose weight, you must decide how many calories you want to burn through exercise and how many to cut by dieting. The same rates for walking away calories apply both to males and females, using each individual's speed, body weight, and frequency of walking to help determine the overall rate. The American Heart Association uses the following rates to estimate how many calories you can burn by walking.

## Calories Burned Per Hour
*(calculated by weight of the walker)*

| Walking Speed | 100 pounds | 150 pounds |
|---|---|---|
| 2 miles per hour | 160 | 240 |
| | *(2.7 cal. per min.)* | *(4 cal. per min.)* |
| 3 miles per hour | 210 | 320 |
| | *(3.5 cal. per min.)* | *(5.3 cal. per min.)* |
| 4.5 miles per hour | 295 | 440 |
| | *(4.9 cal. per min.)* | *(7.3 cal. per min.)* |

## Step 9: *Plan Your Calorie Deficit*

Using the chart just above, decide how long and how fast you want to walk each day. Then calculate the number of calories your walking program will burn. Your body weight may not be on this chart, but you can estimate your calories-per-hour or calories-per-minute based on the weights given. Then use the following equations to decide how your calorie deficit will give you the weight loss you want.

### Calories Used in Each Walk:

$$\underline{\hspace{3cm}} \quad \text{x} \quad \underline{\hspace{3cm}} \quad = \quad \underline{\hspace{3cm}}$$

*(calories per minute)*   *(number of minutes)*   *(calories burned each walk)*

### Calories Burned Each Week by Walking:

$$\underline{\hspace{3cm}} \quad \text{x} \quad \underline{\hspace{3cm}} \quad = \quad \underline{\hspace{3cm}}$$

*(calories burned per walk)*   *(number of walks per week)*   *(calories burned per week)*

### Exercise and Diet Calories:

$$\underline{\hspace{3cm}} \quad \text{x} \quad \underline{\hspace{3cm}} \quad = \quad \underline{\hspace{3cm}}$$

*(weekly calorie*          *(calories burned by*       *(calories to cut*
*deficit—from step 8)*      *walking—from above)*       *by dieting)*

## Step 10: *The Weight Chart*

One final step is essential—a step many do not want to take: Put these figures down in black and white. We can fudge a bit about our progress as long as we only speak in general terms, but there is no room for fudging when it is written down on paper. Writing it down makes it more visible and easier to manage over a long period, and it makes sense to follow this basic principle of management: If you cannot measure it, you cannot manage it.

A chart is the best way to measure and manage a weight-loss program. It may hurt at first to put your current weight on the chart, but it feels awfully good to look back weeks or months later and see how far you have come. A chart that is inhibiting at the start becomes a greater motivator with each successful week of diet and exercise. As the line on the chart moves downward, you can see concrete evidence that pounds are falling off. Once the results start to show, entering the weight from each weekly weigh-in can become a high point of your week.

## Directions for Chart No. 2

There are countless ways to construct weight-loss charts. Graph paper provides a ready-made format and can be purchased almost anywhere school supplies are sold. Simply write a range of weights down the left-hand column, then put the dates for weekly weight checks across the top. Chart 2 shows you how to start:

• Put your current weight at the top of the left side, and then enter weight levels down the left side that decrease in one-pound increments. Along the top, enter the dates for your weekly weigh-ins.

• Draw a line downward from your current weight on the date of the first weigh-in to the weight you want to have on the last weigh-in date. This is your goal line.

• Place a dot on the graph to show your current weight. Then, at the date of your next weigh-in, place a dot at the weight shown for this date. Connect the dots, and you have a visible indication of your progress. This line should, of course, always be below the goal line!

If this ten-step approach to weight loss seems simple, this is because it *is* simple. It is also effective. As long as humans have walked the earth, we have gained or lost weight because of food and exercise. Too much food and too little exercise leads to fat build-up, while less food and more exercise leads to a slimmer, healthier body. No new theories, scientific breakthroughs, or quick-and-easy weight loss programs are as effective as this time tested, repeatedly proven approach. For losing weight and keeping it off, this is the path to success.

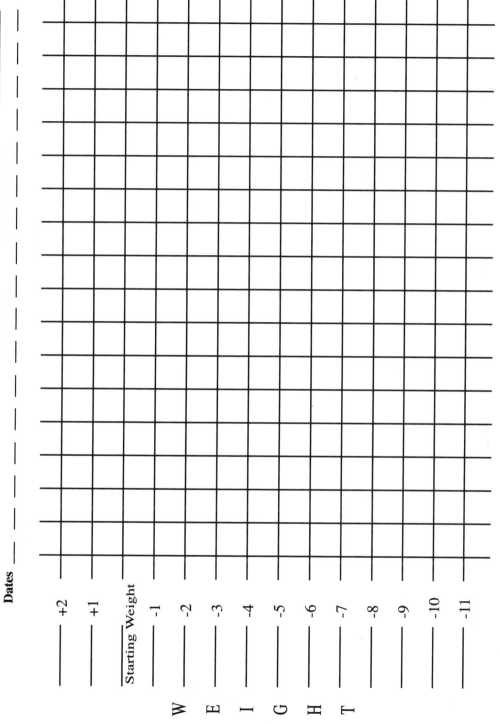

**Months** —— ——

**Dates** —— ——

+2
+1
Starting Weight
-1
-2
-3
-4
-5
-6
-7
-8
-9
-10
-11

W E I G H T

**CHART NO. 2: WEIGHT CHART (FOR WEEKLY WEIGHT LOSS PROGRESS)**

*Chapter Seven*

# When and Where to Walk

*"Make level paths for your feet and take only ways that are firm."*
—*Proverbs 4:26*

There is a time and place for everything, including walking. But many couch potatoes blame a lack of time or place for their failure to exercise. Usually these excuses are just poor rationalization. Setting aside the time to walk takes effort that many are not willing to expend. And, while finding a good, safe, and accessible place to walk may take a little ingenuity, it is within anyone's grasp.

 ## When to Walk

When to walk is a very personal choice. Many walkers begin each day with exercise, others use their lunch hours, and still others unwind with brisk walks after work. Some even enjoy the solitude of walking late at night. While this is a matter of taste, it is a choice that should be made wisely. If you do not choose a time that is right for you, your chances of sticking with an exercise program are slim.

I walk early in the morning. There is something about the freshness of the world in these early hours that energizes me for the rest of the day. Using my walking time for uninterrupted reflection and prayer helps me start each day in close communion with God. It also saves time, since exercising before my morning shower eliminates the need to change into and out of exercise togs later in the day. By the time I dress for work each morning, I feel energized, spiritually centered, and have my exercise out of the way for the day.

Dr. Kenneth Cooper has outlined four optimal times for exercise: early morning, lunch, before the evening meal, and at least ninety minutes after the evening meal. He notes that morning exercisers are more likely to stick to their exercise habit because they are not faced with deciding whether to postpone it when unexpected conflicts develop later.

Many walkers prefer to exercise during their lunch hour, often claiming they could not survive without a midday boost from exercise. Countless executives have told me that exercise in the middle of the business day clears away their mental cobwebs and makes them more effective through their afternoons. One of my former secretaries even kept walking shoes under her desk so she would not waste a minute before hitting the paths at noon each day.

It does not matter *when* you walk, but it does matter *that* you walk. Too many people use lack of time as an excuse for avoiding it altogether. A national opinion survey reported in *Fitness Management* magazine found the most common reason for not exercising is lack of time. While 84 percent of a "less active" group found time to watch at least three hours of television a week, they claimed there was no time for exercise.

Here are a couple of ground rules for choosing a time to walk:

• Do not expect to create time. Find the best time you have available!

• Choose your time wisely. Then commit to use it regularly.

Whatever time you choose to walk, make it a time you will actually use day after day, week after week, month after month. If you pick the wrong time, your chances of dropping out will skyrocket. An exercise program is something in which you will invest thousands of hours, so think carefully about which hours you can best count on to produce long term dividends.

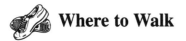 **Where to Walk**

Just as the time you choose for walking will play a big part in the success or failure of your program, so will the place. If it is not safe, pleasant, and easily accessible, you are not likely to keep going there. Again, personal choice comes into play, as do such obvious factors as your geographic location, weather, age, and personal exercise goals. You might be able to just step out the door and walk, but this may not be the best choice.

A great advantage of walking is that it can be done on any smooth, relatively level surface. There is no need for an expensive health club, court, course, or other specialized facility. You can use the streets and sidewalks of the busiest cities, dirt roads that wind through farm land, or suburban lanes that have little traffic. For many walkers the perfect exercise trail is just beyond the front door. Others may have to venture farther from home to find just the right spots, but the odds are that you will not have to travel far.

If you choose to just step out the front door and walk, make sure the conditions are right for you. Personally, I cannot get excited about walking on busy city streets, but I know people who love walking for exercise in the middle of America's busiest cities. They seem to draw energy from the constant hustle and bustle. I admire their enthusiasm, but this is not my idea of a good time. I prefer a quieter, slower atmosphere.

Fortunately my front door opens onto a quiet residential street with a country road just around the corner, so I can wind through neighborhood streets one day and head down the country lane the next. As I write this chapter, for example, I am fresh from a walk past newly plowed cornfields and a pasture in which cattle were quietly grazing. For me, such scenes are food for the soul. For some others, they would be boring. Consider what recharges your own spiritual batteries when you choose the places where you will walk. These surroundings will play a big part in keeping you coming back for more.

## City Walking

If you live in a large city, you may very well enjoy fitness walking alongside the traffic of your busy streets. Many people do. Cities offer much to catch the eye, from rich architectural features in old and new city buildings to the international flavor of ethnic neighborhoods. There are sights, sounds, and smells in a busy city that stimulate the senses, and walking puts you in the middle of the ever changing activity. If this appeals to you and is convenient, you have found your walking spot.

City streets do not come equipped with mileage markers for walkers, but city blocks often serve a similar purpose. In Manhattan, for example, twenty city blocks equal one mile, making it easy for walkers in the Big Apple to keep track of their distance. If the blocks in your city are of uniform size, measure one and then use this distance to figure how many blocks make up a mile. The math is as easy as the exercise itself.

length of a mile (in feet):  <u>5,280</u>
      *divided by*
length of a block (in feet):  <u>      </u>
      *equals*
number of blocks in a mile:  <u>      </u>

One aspect of city walking that cannot be ignored is the danger. Sadly, city streets are not the safest places these days. This does not mean you should avoid them as fitness walking sites, but it does mean you should take some safety precautions before weaving your way into the traffic and crowds.

The best safety precaution is another person—a walking partner. There is safety in numbers, and walking with a spouse or good friend can lower your chances of being disturbed. Having to go alone should not prevent your venturing out, however. Just equip yourself with some basic personal protection items—a police whistle and a small can of pepper spray. Always carry identification, too, and a couple of quarters just in case you need to make a quick phone call. Obviously, city walkers are wise to stay in well traveled areas rather than take the back alleys; and it is best to avoid walking after dark. Using streets just a block or so away from main thoroughfares often works well, since they are almost as safe as the busiest streets but have less noise, pollution, and fewer other pedestrians to dodge.

The need for a few safety precautions should not inhibit anyone from walking on city streets. Safety must be a concern for all walkers, regardless of where they live and walk. More than five thousand pedestrians are killed in America every year, and safety is not just a city concern. Whether in the city, country, or suburbs, it pays to be careful.

## Suburban and Rural Walking

On a recent visit to my hometown, I saw people of all ages out walking for exercise on streets that I had all to myself on visits just a few years earlier. It is the same in communities throughout America, as millions now walk every day in the most convenient of places: their own neighborhood streets. Walking in the neighborhood eliminates the need for driving to a track, keeps you in a familiar environment, gives an increased feeling of safety, and helps you keep up with your neighborhood comings and goings.

Like city streets, residential neighborhoods and rural roads do not have mileage markers, so you must measure your route before beginning if you want to keep track of your mileage. The easiest way is to drive the route and use your car's odometer readings to help identify landmarks at approximately quarter-mile intervals. Jot down these landmarks and use your notes to help you spot them on your first few walks. You will soon have them imbedded in your mind as if they were granite milestones.

Many walkers like to vary their routes from day to day. This is easy to do in residential neighborhoods. If you have measured the quarter-mile segments, you can put them together in countless different ways. For a change of scenery, start out with part of one route, turn onto another for a while, then wind up on yet another as you can let the parts of several routes add up to a completely new one. Most of us always start out in the same direction, so even just reversing that direction can make an old route seem almost completely new. Variety makes walking more fun, and even our own neighborhoods can provide a surprising amount.

If you walk in a residential or rural setting, you may find you have to walk on streets instead of sidewalks, and this demands special attention to safety. The most important safety rule when walking in the street is to always walk facing the oncoming traffic. This increases your awareness of traffic as well as your visibility to drivers. It is also wise to step off the road when cars approach from both directions at once. This is courteous to the drivers and it decreases your chances of being hit. Pedestrians always come out on the short end of collisions with motor vehicles; so do all you can to avoid this kind of collision.

In rural settings, animals can also pose problems. Dogs often are not controlled as well in the country as in the city, and even friendly dogs can be frightening when you do not know them. A walker has no way of telling whether a strange dog is friendly or a threat, so it is always best to assume the worst. I try to steer clear of areas where I know dogs often roam free. If this is a particularly bothersome problem in your area, you might also pick up one of the dog repellent sprays available in pet shops. They are humane and can take care of the problem very well.

 **Fitness Tracks**

There are obvious advantages to walking on tracks built especially for this purpose. They are usually level, almost always have distance markers at least every quarter mile, are safe, and often have absorbent surfaces that actually make walking easier. New tracks are popping up at a rapid rate, built by hospitals, communities, schools, companies, and others anxious to provide safe environments for exercise.

The surfaces of athletic tracks vary widely, from packed dirt to rubberized asphalt. As a rule of thumb, the walking becomes easier as the surface gets springier. Loose sand or dirt, for example, soaks up the energy in each step, while a rubberized surface seems to add energy through a bounce-back effect. Many indoor health clubs and school facilities now feature rubberized asphalt tracks that provide terrific traction and safety. These surfaces are also found on some outdoor tracks, but packed dirt is much more common. Whatever the surface, it will work well if it is smooth, level, well marked, and free of obstacles.

Monotony is the most common criticism of athletic tracks, and is a turnoff to many walkers. Going three miles on a quarter-mile track, for example, means covering the same territory twelve times. This can be boring, but it can also pose the perfect opportunity for putting your body on "automatic pilot" and focusing your mind on other things. For combining reflection and prayer with safe exercise, a circular track can be ideal.

There is probably a track near your home. Many schools open their tracks for community use after school hours. Many hospitals, too, have built health track on their grounds as parts of wellness programs. YMCA and YWCA facilities in many communities have tracks, as do many commercial health clubs—sometimes even indoors. A little checking will probably turn up several nearby alternatives.

## Walking Trails in Parks

Not all tracks are circular. The ones found in parks and greenbelts are often winding and scenic. Throughout America trails are being laid out along river banks, utility rights-of-way, old railway beds, and other out-of-the-way places. Just miles from Capitol Hill in Washington DC, for example, a lovely trail winds through the woods alongside the George Washington Parkway and Potomac River, drawing thousands daily to walk, jog, and ride bikes. In Kingsport, Tennessee, a beautiful greenway beckons walkers to its trails beneath a canopy of trees from the Holston River through the city center. Even in the middle of New York City a scenic trail around the reservoir in Central Park provides a soothing, back-to-nature escape for walkers.

The big city parks are not the only ones with unique and enticing walking trails. You can find great ones in many small communities. Franklin, Tennessee, for example, has a lovely, level, mile-long track that snakes its way through the city park, passing the site of an old fort and circling an enormous wooden play sculpture for children. For shady, back-to-nature walking, such places are hard to beat.

If you want to walk on a prepared trail but not an oval athletic track, there are many from which to choose, and one is probably close to you. Call your local Chamber of Commerce, the Wellness Department of a local hospital, your local American Heart Association office, or some other local organization concerned with health and wellness. With a little detective work, you might find greenways and park trails that you never knew existed in your own community. These are wonderful places for safe walking, for meeting others from the community, and for enjoying the beauty that abounds in America's towns and cities.

##  Mall Walking

You may not think of your local mall as an exercise facility, but millions get their exercise in those sprawling concrete and glass structures every day. Almost every city has at least one shopping mall, and they are all built for one kind of movement —walking. Malls are safe, level, and well lit. They are always kept at a pleasant temperature, and they are free of the threats of bad weather or traffic hazards. They are, in short, superb environments for walking.

Mall operators long ago caught on to the fact that opening their facilities to walkers makes good business sense. After all, their sales depend on how well they can attract people. If they get folks to come and walk, they know that many will stay to shop. They also know that familiarity breeds customer loyalty. Many malls now hand out maps for mall walkers that show the best routes and the locations of mileage markers inside the mall. Some even open their doors early each morning just for mall walking, letting the exercisers make their rounds before the stores open and the corridors become crowded with shoppers.

Fast walkers often shy away from mall walking, feeling that weaving among shoppers is too constraining. This is no problem for those who can walk before the stores open, but it may explain why older walkers make up the bulk of the mall walking army at busier times of the day. For those who need a good, moderate workout, mall walking is ideal. A half hour of moderately brisk walking several times a week gives about three quarters of the benefits you can get from a full athletic routine. With mall walking this can be done indoors, on a flat surface, and free from the safety concerns that go with outdoor walking. Small wonder so many older Americans have made it part of their daily routine!

 **A Change of Pace**

One of the best advantages of walking is its infinite variety. You can do it anywhere and in lots of different ways. The boring sameness that plagues many other exercise activities is just not a factor in walking. Varying your route from day to day can totally change the surroundings, and you can even occasionally add different types of walking to increase the variety.

If you start getting bored with walking on a track at a nearby school or through the streets of your neighborhood, simply try a new spot for a few days. A short drive to a local park can give a dramatic change of scenery, as can going to another neighborhood to walk with a friend. Your walking program can be constantly changing if you look for different routes to walk in your own community and plan special walking opportunities as part of your business and vacation trips.

Watching for special opportunities can yield fascinating experiences. The places you can walk for fitness are limited only by your imagination. Here are a few ideas to get your own creative juices flowing:

| | |
|---|---|
| Botanical Gardens | Arboretums |
| National Parks | Wildlife Preserves |
| National Forests | State Parks |
| Zoos | Self-Guided City Tours |
| Greenbelt Trails | Amusement Parks |
| Historic Sites | Long Bridges |
| Suburban Office Parks | Nature Trails |

Most of these places will have smooth, well-maintained surfaces, but some other superb locations might not. State and national parks usually offer beautiful and bountiful opportunities, but the trails are often much steeper and rougher than regular exercise paths. Hiking is what these trails call for, and this is a very different type of walking. Hiking, however, draws on the same stamina and muscles you develop in daily walks on smoother surfaces, and it can take you to vistas that refresh your spirit while exercising your body.

Whatever the surface and wherever the place, whether hiking deep in a thick forest or striding city streets on a self-guided tour, finding new and different places to walk adds spice to the exercise habit. The variety is a grand advantage of walking that few other forms of exercise can match.

Walking is an exercise loaded with variety. Indoors or out, fast or slow, city or country, short distance or long haul: the choices for making this exercise fit your personal needs and desires are virtually endless. Make these choices for yourself instead of following the dictates of a friend or fitness guru. The more you personalize your walking program, the more enjoyable it will be for you. And the more enjoyable it is, the more likely you are to want to do it day after day after day.

The fraternity of fitness walkers is vast and diverse. An eighty-year-old mall walker has far more in common with a twenty-five-year-old race-walker than most of us would imagine. Their exercise is essentially the same despite the difference in speed, and both get the benefits of better health with little risk of injury. Fitness walking can be as unique as all the more than sixty million Americans who are already doing it. Decide when and where walking will work best for you, and you will have the makings of a pleasant new habit that can last a lifetime.

*Chapter Eight*

# Preparing to Walk

*"Their clothes did not wear out nor did their feet become swollen."*
*—Nehemiah 9:21*

All you really need for walking are two things you were born with: feet. Technically, even shoes are optional, but fitness walking will not be very pleasant without them. Good shoes are all you really need to buy in the way of equipment and clothing, but there are a few other choices that can make it a fuller, more enjoyable experience.

 ## The Right Shoes

Walking for fitness places greater demands on your feet than everyday walking, and these special demands call for special shoes. You do not need to be an expert on walking shoes to find good ones, but a few pointers can help you make a good choice. As the old advertisement for Goodyear tires put it, this is "where the rubber meets the road." The idea is to get shoes that will make your fitness walking easier and more enjoyable, mile after mile.

The old sneakers and loafers in your closet are fine for slow strolls, but do not rely on them for fitness walking. Shoes that are comfortable for walking around the mall or neighborhood often lack the support and other features needed for sustained, brisk walking. Sneakers, for example, usually have crepe soles that heat up and cause uncomfortable perspiration. And comfortable old loafers tend to let your feet slide around, causing major-league blisters when the walking gets fast. Shoes that are made right and fit right can make all the difference.

Most athletic footwear manufacturers have only recently noticed that walkers far outnumber the runners who have been the focus of their attention. But almost every shoe manufacturer now makes shoes specifically for fitness walkers. Many of these walking shoes resemble running shoes, and this is okay up to a point—but the two exercises do not call for exactly the same kinds of shoes.

Running and walking place completely different demands on the feet, so it stands to reason that the shoes would differ for the two sports. Runners crash down hard on their heels, so they need thick cushioning. Walkers do not need as much cushioning, but they need greater firmness to help support the slower shift of weight from heel to toe.

There are now more than two hundred models of walking shoes to choose from, as the old running shoe clones have given way to shoes that are engineered for the specific physical demands of walking. While picking the right ones can make a difference in how you feel about exercising, you rarely encounter much walking expertise among the salespersons in athletic shoe stores. So it pays to know what you are after.

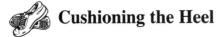 ## Cushioning the Heel

In walking, your heel strikes the ground first, and at a rather steep angle. Since this impact is repeated several thousand times each mile, some cushioning is obviously necessary. Many beginning fitness walkers look for shoes with thick cushions at the heels, but this can be counterproductive. If a heel cushion is too soft it can create a feeling similar to walking on loose sand—where your foot sinks into the surface as you try to move forward. This works against the natural walking gait and quickly results in tired legs. Heels that are too thick can also cause soreness, forcing your toes down too fast and causing a "toe slap" that pulls your shin muscles. You need enough cushioning to provide reasonable comfort and help support your foot as your weight rolls forward—but too much cushioning will work against your natural movement.

Choose a shoe with a fairly low, beveled heel, and your foot will roll down smoothly and naturally. Women who wear high-heeled shoes know very well how high heels alter the natural walking gait. High heels force short steps, while low heels allow a longer, more natural stride. You should choose a walking shoe with cushion about ½- to ¾-inch above the sole. This will provide a comfortable cushion without altering your basic gait.

 ## Controlling the Heel

At the heel, stability is actually more important than cushioning. So look for walking shoes with a good "heel counter"—a stiff support band that will keep your heel stable. Heel counters are usually made of plastic and are easy to spot on the outside of the shoes, wrapping around the heel and often extending several inches along each side.

Most of us do not walk in a perfectly straight line. About 95 percent of us tend to step on the outsides of our heels and roll our feet to the inside as we move forward. This is called "pronation." Most of the other 5 percent land on the inside of the heels, rolling our feet to the outside, a pattern called "supination." Neither pattern causes much trouble in everyday walking, but either one can spell trouble for fitness walkers if it is excessive.

A little pronation can act as a sort of natural shock absorber, but too much can cause big problems. It can torque joints all the way up the leg, straining and often injuring ankles, knees, and hips. This is such a common problem that sports doctors often look first at a patient's athletic shoes when diagnosing knee complaints. If the shoes show pronounced wear on the outside of the heels there is a very good chance that excessive pronation is the root of the knee pain. For many, new shoes are the only treatment needed.

Two things help control pronation and supination: a bit of firmness and a good heel counter. Heel counters are also found on good running shoes, but they are longer on walking shoes, often reaching almost to the middle of a shoe along the inside. Check this part of a shoe carefully when you are shopping. If you do not see a good, firm heel counter, look for another model.

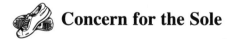 ## Concern for the Sole

The soles of walking shoes should be more than just platforms for your feet. Well designed soles help support your weight as it moves forward, assisting as your load shifts through each step. The shoe's heel should be beveled to absorb the angle at which your heel strikes the ground, and the midsection should be curved to follow the rocking motion as you shift your weight, with the toe slightly raised to help you push off onto your next step.

The midsole is the foundation of a good walking shoe. It is the part of the sole that is thickest, above the rubber outside sole but below the upper portion of the shoe. A good midsole should cushion, protect, and help put some spring in your steps; but too much cushioning can interfere with natural rebounding. This makes the feet and leg muscles tire quickly, tending to cut short both your mileage and enthusiasm.

When you select a walking shoe, give the midsole a squeeze test. Hold the shoe so your thumb is beneath the outersole and your forefinger is above the midsole (along the outside of the shoe), then squeeze. If the midsole compresses to less than half its original thickness, it is probably too soft. If it does not compress at all—or very little—it is probably too stiff. This is a good preliminary test, but the real test is how the shoe feels when you actually try it on. If your foot feels squishy inside the shoe as you take some trial steps, look for another shoe.

 ## The Toe Box

Be sure you have plenty of room at the toes of your walking shoes. You need this room because your forefoot flattens out and your toes spread wide when your weight moves to the front of your foot. Because this happens with each step in walking, most good walking shoes feature a wide toe box.

The toe box is a reinforced area at the toe of the shoe. It usually blends into the overall shape of the shoe, but you can feel its firmness from both the inside and the outside of the shoe. The toe box should be high enough to give your toes plenty of clearance, and wide enough to let them spread out naturally. If you try on a shoe that is so tight you cannot wiggle your toes, put it back on the shelf. You are inviting corns, calluses, and other unnecessary aches and pains if you wear walking shoes with a tight toe box.

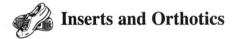 ## Inserts and Orthotics

Look inside a walking shoe, and you will usually find some form of padded insert. They can be as simple as sock-liners or as sophisticated as contoured, removable inserts. These serve varying functions, mainly helping keep your feet in proper position and working with the outersole to cushion the impact of your steps.

Removable inserts look much like arch supports that you can buy in most drug stores, but they are designed specifically for walkers. In better shoes they will be made of multi-density material—soft material on top for cushioning and harder supportive material along the bottom. The additional padding and better fit that good inserts provide can do a lot to make your walks more comfortable.

For most of us, the devices that are included in the shoes are all we need. But some walkers need the extra help of specialized inserts designed to help with specific problems and needs. Such inserts are called "orthotics." You can buy basic orthotics over the counter to help your feet and legs do their work, and more specialized ones can be made to meet individual needs. If you have recurring problems with feet or legs, you should have a podiatrist examine your feet to determine whether you need prescription orthotics. Prescription orthotics are usually made from cast molds of your feet, with special wedging at the front or rear to improve stability. They slip into your walking shoes to replace the original inserts, essentially giving you walking shoes that are tailor made.

 ## Where to Find Walking Shoes

The last time I needed a new pair of walking shoes, I went about selecting a new model very scientifically. I studied manufacturers' brochures, checked the experts' opinions about which models were best, and reviewed all the features of various shoes. By the time I went to the store to actually purchase the shoes, I knew exactly what I wanted. But I ran into one unexpected problem: When I put those shoes on my feet, they felt awful! The construction was excellent, the features appealing, and the shoe was made by a manufacturer whose shoes I had worn quite happily before; but this particular model simply did not fit my own feet well.

Despite construction and technical features in walking shoes, nothing should ever take precedence over the way a shoe feels on your own foot. This is something no advertisement, salesperson, or store display can decide for you. You can evaluate it only by trying on shoes, walking in them, and asking yourself whether you really want to spend hundreds of hours with them on your feet.

If the walking shoes do not fit and feel right in the store, do not take them home. Good walking shoes should never need a break-in period—what you feel is what you get. As you walk around the store, try to simulate the way you will actually walk in the shoes. Wear thick athletic socks like those you will wear for your regular walking, and walk around the store in the shoes for as long as necessary. Take several long strides, and do not worry about looking funny or appearing overly picky. This is serious business that may take a while, and it is time well spent.

If you are lucky you may find a salesperson who is up to speed on what makes a good walking shoe, but do not count on it. Shoe salespersons are usually far more well versed on running shoes and basketball shoes than on walking shoes. So it makes sense to do some advance thinking about what is available, what you should look for, and what you really need. The ratings in *Consumer Reports* and *Walking* magazine's annual "shoe review" issue are good references. With a little preparation you will probably be the most authoritative voice on walking shoes in the entire store.

## Tips for Shoe Shopping

The following diagram shows some things to look for when you visit your athletic shoe store.

### What to Look for in a Walking Shoe

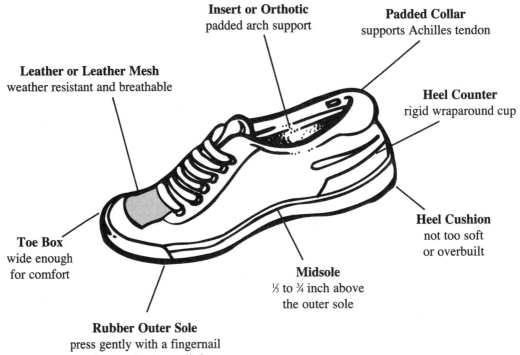

## Dress for Success

Most sports require an arsenal of bats, balls, rackets, helmets, pads, or other special-ized equipment—but walking does not. All it takes is energy and a good pair of walking shoes. Everything else is optional. You probably already have clothes that will work perfectly, but there are plenty of sports stores, catalogs, and Web sites loaded with special clothes and accessories in case you want to go all out.

You can wear almost anything for walking, but some clothes work better than others. Comfort is the key, and what is comfortable will vary from season to season and person to person. Just as it pays to "dress for success" in the business world, it pays to dress for fitness success when you walk.

 ## Socks

New fitness walkers sometimes try to keep their feet cooler by not wearing socks. Big mistake! In hot weather, wearing socks may seem like overkill—especially since the insides of walking shoes often feel so soft. But wear them anyway. Without socks your feet can become uncomfortably wet, slide around inside your shoes, and cause blisters. Take a long, brisk walk without socks, and you can count on finding blisters and red spots when you shed your shoes.

Feet sweat, and without socks the sweat has nowhere to go. Some walking shoes advertise that their interior linings wick away perspiration, but this is not enough. Each foot can produce close to a cup of perspiration every day, and good socks are essential to absorb it.

Good socks can actually extend the life of your shoes, too. Since almost half of a foot's perspiration stays inside the shoe, it will go into the lining and insole if not properly wicked away. This can cause excess wear, fraying, drying, cracking, and curling throughout the shoe's interior, thus aging the shoe too quickly, making it less comfortable, and severely shortening its life.

The fabric you choose in athletic socks is a matter of personal preference, though cotton is the most popular by far. Some walkers are devoted to wool socks, especially for winter, because wool can absorb up to 70 percent of its weight in water. But many people feel an uncomfortable itch when wool is next to their skin. You can also pick from silk, synthetics, and blends of all kinds. Double-layered socks of a cotton/Orlon blend are particularly good, though they are often hard to find. For beginners it is wise to try several different types before stocking up, and cotton or cotton blend athletic socks are probably the best with which to start.

Some of the cheapest athletic socks you will find are tube socks, but price is about their only advantage. You will not get a good fit from a tube-type sock, and a good fit is too important to sacrifice. Hold a tube sock up alongside a fitted sock, and compare both to the shape of your foot. This tells the story better than I ever could.

As you browse through athletic shoe stores you may see special "walking socks" with padding in the heels and toes to provide an extra cushion. These are comfortable but costly, and the extra padding is not necessary. Good walking shoes will give you all the padding you really need. Wear the special padded socks if you like the way they feel and do not mind the extra cost, but recognize that a couple of drawbacks come along with the added cushioning: tighter shoes caused by the extra padding and more sweat caused by reduced air circulation inside the shoes.

Like shoes, the right socks are ultimately the ones that feel best on your feet. The most important thing to remember about socks is to wear them. Beyond this, consider absorbency, fit, and comfort. If you are wearing socks that feel good and you have neither blisters nor excessive perspiration buildup in your shoes, you have chosen wisely.

## 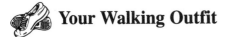 Your Walking Outfit

There are no dress codes for fitness walking. You can wear anything, and people do. Some walkers dress as though they are running a marathon, while others wear neckties or dresses for their daily walks. Wear whatever you like, but realize that some outfits are definitely more comfortable for walking than others.

It is a good idea to think of your walking as a workout—not just a stroll in the park—regardless of how fast or slowly you walk. Fitness walking is regular, serious exercise, and putting on athletic clothing when you do it can help you keep this idea firmly in mind. "Suiting up" to go walk helps get you in an exercise frame of mind and makes you feel more like the athlete that you are.

In choosing walking clothes, make freedom of movement your top consideration. Old jeans that feel great around the house can feel unbelievably restrictive after a couple of miles of fast walking, and skirts that thrash the legs with each step can make it next to impossible for women to keep up a good walking stride. Athletic clothing is the best choice by far.

Fortunately, good athletic clothing is not expensive. Sweatpants, sweatshirts, shorts and T-shirts are all relatively inexpensive, come in a rainbow of colors, and cover the size gamut. It is hard to walk ten feet in a mall without passing a display of T-shirts, and any that are made of cotton or a cotton blend should serve you well. Sweatshirts and sweatpants, too, can be found everywhere from discount stores to boutiques, and almost all will do the job. These are usually made of knitted cotton or a cotton blend with fleecy insides for comfort and absorbency, and they do a good job of letting air in and letting perspiration out.

Some fabrics simply do not breathe. They are so tightly woven that air cannot easily pass through them, preventing perspiration from escaping and evaporating. Inevitably, such fabrics cause heat to build up inside the clothing and resulting discomfort. With so many good, breathable fabrics to choose from, there is no reason a fitness walker should wear clothes that do not enhance the experience.

Comfort is paramount. When you try on walking clothes, move around in them. Do not just look at how they appear in the mirror. Walk around the store, swinging your arms as you will when walking, and bend over as you will while warming up. If the clothes feel too tight in the store, imagine how they will feel several miles down the road. Reject any that are too tight under the arms, bind at the waist, ride up, or in any other way constrict your freedom of movement. You will spend a lot of time in those clothes, and a little effort in picking the right outfits can ensure that these are happy, comfortable hours.

##  Hot Weather Clothing

The basic summer outfit for most fitness walkers is shorts and a T-shirt, but hesitancy to wear shorts should never be an excuse for not exercising. Light, loose fitting cotton pants will do nicely, as will culottes and very loose skirts for women. Look for light colors, porous fabrics, and good freedom of movement. You can enjoy all the benefits of fitness walking whatever your preferences for exposure and style.

A good hat is another must for hot, sunny weather. Lightweight hats and caps with wide brims can shade your face and keep the sun off, which is important both for comfort and for good health. The sun's effects account for 90 percent of all skin cancer, and there are more than 75,000 new cases in America each year. This should be reason enough for anyone to avoid unneeded exposure. Visors provide many of the same benefits as hats, although they do not protect the scalp itself, and many walkers find them more comfortable because of their greater air circulation. Whichever you prefer, it is a good idea to use something to shield your face from the sun's direct rays if you choose to walk during the sunniest times of day.

##  Cold Weather Clothing

How to dress for cold weather walking is more complex. You obviously need more clothes to fight off the cold, but you do not want to be so weighed down that you cannot walk comfortably.

The key word in dressing for cold weather walking is layering. Several layers of relatively thin fabric can actually keep you warmer than one very heavy coat. Each layer is a barrier to the cold, and warm air gets trapped between the layers. As your body warms up with the exercise, the trapped air heats up and, since it is closest to your body, provides a natural insulation. Your body generates plenty of heat, and you can put it to good use by dressing in layers.

There are many other ways to help beat the cold weather. A good scarf, for example, will protect your neck, chin, and mouth from chilly breezes. And, as most of the body's heat escapes through the head, it makes sense to close off that escape route with a hat. Earmuffs can be worth their weight in gold, and the need for gloves or mittens is obvious.

For winter walking it is better to overdress than to underdress. You will get warmer as you walk, and you can always remove a jacket or shirt to tie around your waist. Dress to be warm at the start, and be prepared to shed a layer if necessary.

## Wet Weather Clothing

Some people do not have sense enough to come in out of the rain, and this certainly applies to some fitness walkers. Many will stay indoors if there is a cloud anywhere nearby, but others will walk outdoors whether it is sunny or pouring. If you fall in the latter category, be sure you stay healthy by dressing for the wet weather.

A jacket is the basic piece of a walker's rainwear, and it should be both waterproof and breathable. Nonporous fabrics can trap heat and sweat inside while keeping the water outside, and this is not a great trade off. The parka-style jacket is especially practical, providing excellent body coverage and often including a hideaway hood to cover the head. Whatever style you choose, though, get a rain jacket large enough to wear over another jacket or sweatshirt so you can use it in cold weather as well as warm.

A rain jacket takes care of the top half of your body, but you are not likely to enjoy your walking if the rest of your body is soaked. If you plan to be an all-weather walker, rain pants will come in handy. These are loose pants designed to be worn over shorts or sweatpants, and should be made of the same kind of material used in your jacket—breathable and waterproof. Since the pants are often sold in sets with jackets, getting the right match is easy. Many walkers try to economize by skipping the pants, only to return for some after the first good rain leaves them with drenched shorts or sweatpants.

For a rain hat, choose anything that has a brim wide enough to keep rain out of your eyes and fits well enough to stay on in a breeze. Many walkers bypass the hat and rely on the zip-out hoods that are built into their parkas. This works fine for keeping the water out, but parka hoods can interfere with your peripheral vision. If you are walking where traffic is a factor, this can be a good reason to choose a hat rather than a hood.

All in all the best guideline for how to dress when fitness walking is to use your own common sense. If it is hot, dress to stay as cool as possible, and do the reverse if it is cold. As for dressing to walk in the rain, the best idea actually is to look for a good indoor alternative. With indoor tracks and treadmills so prevalent, there is simply no need for this kind of discomfort. With a little forethought, it is easy to "dress for success" in your fitness walking.

##  Health and Safety Items

Fitness walking is as safe as an exercise can get, but no exercise is completely without risk. There are some things you can do to minimize the possibility of pain or problems, and "using your own common sense" tops the list. Just remember what you already know: Avoid dangerous places, always walk facing traffic, and come inside if it is too hot or too cold. Let caution be your guide, but also consider some of the optional equipment that can help make your walking healthier and safer.

### A Fanny Pack

This is not the most essential piece of walking equipment, but it tops the optional list because it enables you to carry so many others. "Fanny pack" is the name commonly used for pouches designed to be worn around the waist. You might also see them advertised as "waist packs." These have room for most of the items you might want or need on a long walk.

Backpacks serve the same purpose and are often used by hikers and cross-country skiers, but they are much bulkier and heavier. The beauty of the fanny pack is that it does not restrict your movement in any way. With no straps or weight on the shoulders, your arms can swing normally as you stride along. Yet the pouch has room for identification, insect repellent, pepper spray, sunglasses, sunblock, and other nice-to-have items. You can find good, inexpensive fanny packs in most sporting goods departments.

## Identification

When one of my friends was visiting a military base several years ago, he found a deserted road just perfect for his early morning exercise. He had gone a couple of miles one morning around sunrise when he was stopped by security guards and asked what he was doing in an area marked "off limits." Unfortunately he was not carrying any identification, so he spent an embarrassing hour trying to prove he was not a spy. You may never have this kind of bad luck, but you still should never head out to exercise without some form of identification.

At minimum, when you go out walking always carry your name, address, telephone number, blood type, and notice of any special medical condition. This will give vital information to emergency workers in the unlikely event that you fall victim to an accident or medical emergency. It is not important what form your identification takes, but—in the words of an American Express commercial—"Don't leave home without it!"

## Sunblock

Each year more than 75,000 people are diagnosed with skin cancer, and about 5,800 people die of the disease. This problem increases as people focus on developing beautiful tans and ignore the long-term skin damage that comes with them. Having gone through two skin-cancer surgeries, I am probably more attuned to this threat than most. But medical studies publicized in recent years should have made the danger of too much sun obvious to everyone by now. Sun damage to the skin is a rampant problem, but the good news is that most of it can be prevented.

Avoiding sun damage just takes spending a few bucks for some good sunblock, then remembering to use it. Choose a product that offers a sun protection factor (SPF) of 15 or higher. When you walk for forty-five minutes or so on a sunny day, you can easily get too much sun. Make a habit of putting sunblock on exposed skin—particularly around your face and neck—before venturing out. This will lower your chances of being among the millions who will develop some form of skin cancer. As a bonus you will also escape the sun's drying effects that age the skin faster than necessary.

## Blister Resisters

The most common problem for fitness walkers is the blister. These are caused by friction against toes or feet, and they usually begin as hot spots. If nothing is done to stop the friction, these develop into fluid-filled sacs between skin layers that can be very painful. They can also become infected if they are severe enough and go untreated. It is a good idea to carry something along to use if a hot spot starts to develop.

Spreading a little petroleum jelly between your toes is the easiest way to prevent blisters from developing. This can eliminate the rubbing that starts the hot spots if you apply it before starting out, and it can stop the friction if you catch the problem in time while on the trail. The same solution can eliminate or stop chafing on the insides of the legs, a problem some heavier walkers might encounter from time to time.

Walking is too pleasant an experience to be spoiled by minor inconveniences such as blisters, tight shoes, or clothing that does not move as freely as you. Though the only required equipment for this exercise is your body, choose your optional extras carefully, and you can make your walking workouts as pleasant as they are effective.

*Chapter Nine*

# Learning to Walk

*"Teach me your way, O Lᴏʀᴅ, and I will walk in your truth."*
*—Psalm 86:11*

At first glance, instructions on how to walk may seem completely unnecessary. Walking is something most of us have been doing since the time we blew out the candles on our first birthday cakes. But walking just to get around is not quite the same as walking for fitness, and a quick look at the differences can prevent your starting off on the wrong foot.

There is no great learning curve in fitness walking. The technique is essentially the same as for the kind of walking we do every day. But most of us have developed some bad walking habits over our lifetimes. To get the most out of fitness walking, we must break these old habits and replace them with new and better techniques. For the most part this means making minor adjustments and simply paying some attention to a few things we normally take for granted.

Fitness walking should be smooth rather than jerky, and several factors can impede our ability to walk smoothly. Some are physical defects, but most result from bad habits—posture and movement that seem comfortable but that cause us to move awkwardly and less efficiently than we should. Barriers to smooth walking rarely require medical attention. Most are just bad habits that can be corrected by a few minor adjustments.

Volumes have been written about the mechanics of walking. Anthropologists have scrutinized how the human gait has changed over the centuries. Physiologists have studied the movements of every bone, muscle, and ligament in the human body — recording in detail the rationale for why we move as we do. Medical research has diagnosed about every conceivable defect in the skeletal structure, cataloging the barriers that might impede smooth movement. There have been enough scientific studies about walking to make anyone's eyes glaze over.

When you cut through all the technicalities, one conclusion is clear: There is really no big trick to walking. You just put one foot ahead of the other and move forward. Most of us have been doing this all our lives, and it works fine for getting us from place to place. The same technique works for exercise, too, with a few guidelines.

 ## Posture

"Stand up straight and tall!" This is what my father often told me when I was a slouchy teenager, and it was good advice. Little did he know, though, that he was emphasizing one of the key points for fitness walking. The biggest mistakes by new exercise walkers usually involve posture, and these mistakes can cause problems ranging from interference with a comfortable, brisk pace to actual pain.

Most people who begin walking for exercise want to walk fast, so they lean forward, thrust their shoulders ahead of their bodies, and focus their eyes on the ground about three feet ahead. This gives a feeling of movement, of leaning into each step, and it creates the illusion of doing it right. This is just an illusion, however. In reality, this kind of posture amounts to slouching. It prevents the body from being able to move as briskly as it should, and it can lead to one of the few walking related injuries: lower back pain.

The strain that poor walking posture places on your back muscles is easy to experience even without actually walking. To feel it, stand up straight and lean forward from your waist. Let your shoulders slump forward, then move your head out beyond your shoulders, tilted ahead and down. You should feel an big increase in the pressure on your lower back where the spine curves inward. Bad posture forces this fragile focal point to support weight that should be supported by your strong legs and hips, and staying in this position for a long walk can cause recurring lower back pain that is as unnecessary as it is uncomfortable.

Marionettes, the Howdy Doody type of puppets that are suspended from strings, are good images to use in checking posture. The movement of a marionette's hands, feet, and other body parts are all controlled by individual strings, but the most critical string— attached to the top of the marionette's head—controls its posture. When this string is loosened the puppet's whole body slumps downward. When the string is pulled tight the puppet's body springs to attention with head erect, shoulders high, back straight, and all parts in perfect alignment.

To assume the right posture for walking, pretend a giant string is attached to the top of your head. Imagine it is being pulled tight, almost lifting you off the ground, and you should feel the same perfect alignment as the marionette. This is the best posture for walking, and if there is an almost perfect line from your ears to your ankles, you are doing it right.

It is not always easy to maintain good posture while walking, but you can do it by using your head. We have a natural tendency to slouch when we get tired, but it is almost impossible to slouch if your head is up and facing forward. Focus your eyes on the path thirty to forty feet ahead instead of just a few paces ahead. This will prevent your gaze from shifting downward, will keep your head up, and will hold your whole body in alignment. It will also allow you see more of God's beautiful creation all around you.

This last part—looking at the loveliness all around—is among the most pleasant features of fitness walking. The pace is right for enjoying a passing scene that can be truly inspirational. Whether on city streets or deep in the woods, the vistas are all far too good to miss by letting bad posture drag our eyes down to the dusty road. Looking up, looking out, and drinking in the world around us helps maintain good posture while also bringing into clearer focus the beauty all around us.

 **Stride**

The walking stride is simple, and it can be smooth and efficient at any age or speed. Unlike running, which consists of repeatedly thrusting the whole body into the air for forward motion, walking is a cycle of continuous, fluid movements. At least one foot is always on the ground in walking, so the stride is just a process of transferring the body's weight from one foot to the other and moving forward.

Here is essentially what should happen with each step: You straighten your leading leg at the knee and reach forward with it until your heel strikes the ground. Then as your body moves forward over this foot, you transfer your weight from the heel to the outside of the sole. Your other leg, having left the ground, reaches forward to prepare for the next step. As your body moves forward, your weight shifts to the inside of the foot that is on the ground until your toes accept all of your weight. By then your other leg is out front with its ankle bent upward. As the heel of this foot touches the ground, you push off with the toes of the first foot and start the whole process over again. We do this thousands of times every day without thinking about it—and we do not really have to spend much time thinking about it when we walk for exercise, either.

The most important difference in the fitness walking stride is keeping the legs straight at certain times. When you plant your heel on the ground to receive your body's full weight, your knee should be straight and your leg should be fully extended forward. Then your leg should stay straight as it takes all your weight and passes beneath your body. Otherwise, if your leading leg bends at the knee, you will tend to land on your sole instead of on your heel, causing you to bob up and down instead of striding along smoothly. Bending the leading leg instead of keeping it straight is a common problem, but it can easily be overcome. Remember to keep your leg straight to prevent the bobbing motion, allow you to move faster, and quickly develop an important fitness walking habit.

The distance between your feet also contributes to a good stride, because your stride becomes longer as your feet come as close as possible to being in a straight line. To see how this works, try walking several steps forward with your feet spaced about twelve inches apart, side to side. Then try several more steps with your feet about four inches apart, side to side. Finally, try a few steps of putting one foot almost directly in front of the other. You should find your stride lengthening each time you shorten the distance between your feet. This is why race walkers try to keep their feet moving in an almost straight line, stretching their stride by keeping one foot precisely behind the other. For most fitness walkers a four-inch separation is about right. This allows a good long stride without feeling at all unnatural.

One of the most common mistakes of new fitness walkers is trying to gain speed by lengthening the stride beyond what feels normal and comfortable. This is the wrong approach. The right stride length is a matter of how you are built—not how much you exert yourself. As a general rule you will have a short stride if you have short legs and a longer stride if you have long legs. The important thing is to cycle from one foot to the next with a rhythm that brings smooth, efficient movement to your natural stride.

##  Arm Swing

We walk on our legs, but our arms play a much bigger part in walking than most of us realize. They are the secret for increasing speed, and they can help turn walking into a total body exercise. All we have to do is bend our arms instead of keeping them straight. If you go out for a casual stroll, it really does not matter what you do with your arms. You can even keep your hands in your pockets. A natural rhythm develops when you let your arms hang loosely and swing naturally, however, and this rhythm helps the whole process.

In normal walking, your right arm will swing forward at the same time your left leg swings forward, and your left arm will move in synchronization with your right leg. Your arms are like two big pendulums attached to your shoulders, and they counterbalance the movements of two other long pendulums, your legs. Unless you force them to do otherwise, they will naturally swing back and forth in perfect arcs.

Most exercise walkers swing their arms naturally until they are taught a better way. It is often a big surprise to new fitness walkers that how they swing their arms actually affects how swiftly and smoothly they can walk. The change that is needed is not difficult or complex, but it can make an enormous difference. It is just a matter of bending the arms instead of keeping them straight.

When you bend your arms at ninety-degree angles, your arm swing is much faster than when your arms remain straight. There are two reasons. First, by bending your arms you shorten dramatically the length of the pendulum, and the laws of physics tell us that shorter pendulums swing faster than longer ones. Second, bending your arms removes the weight of your hands and forearms from the end of the pendulum. The shorter, lighter arm pendulums start swinging faster, and a signal is telegraphed down to the legs, telling them to pick up the pace. The result is that both arms and legs both move faster, increasing your walking speed. Since walking faster gives a better aerobic workout, most serious fitness walkers use a bent-arm swing.

## Bent-arm Swing

Extend each arm swing back so your hand reaches just beyond and behind your buttocks.

Bring each front arm swing up across the front of your body, reaching your chest.

If you use a bent-arm swing, tighten your arm muscles, and pump your arms as you walk, you can turn your walking into more of a total body workout. Arm pumping requires more strength and control than arm swinging because it is conscious, constant exercise and not just the natural, balancing swing. It almost doubles the aerobic benefits, burning more calories and exercising muscles in the arms, shoulders, and upper and lower back. This increases the amount of energy involved, increasing the intensity of the exercise and getting your whole body into the act.

The bent-arm swing is easy to master. Just bend your elbows into ninety-degree angles, form your hands into loose fists, and swing your arms with natural rhythm— just pumping them more forcefully. On the front swing your hand should go up and across your chest to about the middle. Then your arm should move backward on a back-swing, with your elbows staying close to your body, and stop when the fist reaches back just beyond the buttocks. You may feel that your arms are swinging much further this way than with a regular arm swing, but the distance is actually about the same. The differences are in speed and in the involvement of your upper body. Both increase the intensity of the exercise, and this is a big plus for many walkers.

The biggest drawback to the bent-arm swing is that it looks funny, and you may feel a bit self-conscious when you first try it. It looks a lot like the technique used by race walkers, and this technique is viewed as comical by people who do not realize how much athletic intensity this sport involves. Race walkers long ago learned that the arms can be a secret of success. They walk with their arms bent, tucked close to their bodies, and swinging in aggressive arcs.

Some fitness walkers who want good workouts but do not want to draw attention to themselves compromise by leaving their arms extended but still pump them as aggressively as if they were bent. This is, indeed, a compromise. It is better for fitness than a simple arm swing, but it will not bring the improvements in speed and workout intensity that come with the hard pumping bent-arm swing. If you are really serious about walking for fitness, bend your arms and do it right.

 **Intensity**

How intensely you choose to walk is up to you. Your speed will depend on your age, physical condition, individual goals, and many other factors. But one of the wonderful things about walking is that it offers benefits at every pace—from an evening stroll to competitive race walking. It all depends on who you are, what you want to achieve, and how much energy you wish to expend. For the maximum benefits, however, to your health you must walk intensely enough to elevate your heart rate. This will be discussed in greater detail in chapter 11.

Walking speed is usually measured either in miles per hour or in minutes per mile. If humans were equipped with speedometers, I would prefer the miles per hour measurement. Since we do not come with this equipment, I prefer to talk in terms of minutes per mile. To measure your walking speed this way, simply measure a one-mile distance and then time how long it takes to walk it. Digital sports watches with split-second stopwatch capability are cheap, and they make this kind of measurement easy. Some walkers do not bother keeping track of time or mileage, but most do. Personally, I like to keep track of my progress, so I time each walk to see how long I have exercised and how my speed compares to previous walks.

There are three basic walking speeds: strolling; brisk walking; and race walking. Some walking books divide these speeds further, and different writers and clinicians tend to give the speeds unique and catchy names. When you cut through the jargon, however, these are the three basic choices.

## Strolling

Strolling is easy walking. It is what we do all the time, from shopping to walking the dog to wandering hand-in-hand with a loved one. From a technical point of view strolling is low-intensity exercise. Its speed range runs about twenty to thirty minutes per mile—two to three miles per hour, if you prefer this measurement. This speed is not intense enough to be an aerobic workout, but it can still contribute to fitness in many ways. It burns more calories than staying sedentary, helps your blood circulation, and gives your muscles some exercise—to name just a few of the benefits.

For many older adults, physically-challenged persons, and those rehabilitating from disease or surgery, strolling may be the fastest walking that is reasonable. If so, go for it! It may not be a fast-paced aerobic workout, but it is certainly better than succumbing to the temptation to stay glued to the couch. Anything that gets you up, out, and exercising on a regular basis is good for fitness, and strolling definitely qualifies.

No special technique is needed for strolling. The posture, stride, and arm swing techniques used in more vigorous walking can and should be used in strolling to the greatest extent possible, but they are not necessary. The object here is basic exercise, and you do not have to change old habits to get it. If your knees are not straight at heel-plant or your arms swing at your sides instead of being bent, it is no big deal. The main idea is to simply get out and walk regularly.

When I was a small boy, an elderly woman on our street was considered eccentric because she walked for an hour or so every day. Summer or winter we would see her pass on her daily walks through the neighborhood, into town, and back again. This was long before the fitness craze swept America, and she was a local curiosity. But she staunchly maintained that walking was healthy and that others would be wise to follow her example. She was right. She lived a long, independent life while many of her more sedentary peers died or were forced to move into nursing homes. Even at a strolling pace she reaped the enormous benefits of walking.

## Brisk Walking

Brisk walking is what most serious exercise walkers do. Fitness is its primary goal, so it involves a much faster pace than strolling. Technically, it is a moderate intensity exercise, and its speed range runs from about ten to twenty minutes per mile—three to six miles per hour, if you prefer this measurement. Even at the slow end of its speed range, brisk walking produces numerous health benefits. At the fast end it qualifies solidly as an aerobic workout.

New fitness walkers can plug in at whatever speed feels comfortable, work on the basic walking technique, and increase speed and intensity as weeks and months go by. Many never aspire to walk ten-minute miles, but most healthy walkers can comfortably progress to at least a thirteen- or fourteen-minute mile. At this rate, they can cover 2.5 miles in about thirty-five minutes—a heart and lung workout that easily qualifies as aerobic exercise.

A good walking technique is more important for brisk walking than for casual strolling. Posture, the width between the feet, the straightness of the legs, and the bent-arm swing are all important factors in lengthening your stride and increasing your speed.

To reach the faster end of the brisk-walking speed range, the bent-arm swing is especially important. It not only adds speed but increases the intensity of the exercise by getting upper-body muscles into the act. Pumping your arms will help pick up the pace, spread the exercise benefit through more of your body, and raise the heat in your calorie-burning furnace. If you want to get the most out of your walking and can stand a tougher physical workout, brisk walking is the way to go.

## Race Walking

Race walking is something entirely different, as different from regular walking as sprinting is from jogging. Although it is not widely popular in the United States, this highly demanding competitive sport has an immense following in other countries. Race walking is very high intensity exercise, with a speed range from about 10 minutes per mile to about 5.5 minutes per mile—6-10-plus miles per hour, for those who prefer this measurement. It goes beyond just aerobic exercise, and it requires extremely good physical condition.

Race walking is actually somewhat unnatural, because it involves forcing the body to walk at speeds that more naturally call for running. Somewhere around five or six miles per hour, the body tends to shift gears and switch from walking to running. Race walkers do not allow this to happen. Instead, they modify their stride, leg-swing, and arm-swing to increase their speed without actually running. Runners leap forward so that both feet are, at times, simultaneously off the ground. This is not allowed in race walking.

One of the two basic race-walking rules is that at least one foot must be on the ground at all times. This prevents competitors from using steps that would actually constitute jogging or running. The other basic rule is that the knee of the leading leg must be straight when the heel contacts the ground, and then remain straight until the knee passes under the body. In competitive races, which normally cover from 10 kilometers (6.2 miles) up to 50 kilometers (31.1 miles), race walkers are carefully watched by judges to ensure they abide by these two rules. If they violate either, they are pulled from the race and disqualified on the spot.

Most walkers—myself included—never intend to become race walkers, but this does not mean we cannot learn a lot from the race walking technique. We borrow the hard pumping, bent-arm swing of race walkers to enhance the benefits of brisk walking, for example, and we can gain other useful insights on increasing speed and intensity from studying race-walking techniques. Straight posture, arms bent to ninety degrees and swung close to the body, leading legs kept unbent from impact through most of the stride, and steps so narrow they are almost in a straight line—all these are essential for race walkers. These are also good techniques for fitness walkers who use the slower, brisk-walking pace.

These adjustments can help increase walking speed, but they also give race walkers a unique look that many onlookers find amusing. By flexing the pelvis with each step and keeping the feet in a straight line to lengthen the stride, a race walker's movement produces a distinctive wiggle. On these rare occasions when race walking receives media coverage, this wiggle usually attracts feeble attempts at humor by announcers who know little about the sport or the athletic ability it requires.

If you press your fitness walking to the fast end of the brisk-walking range, you well may want to try some race-walking techniques. It may also be a test of courage, however, since the race walkers' wiggle is sure to attract attention. I enjoy experimenting with it in short spurts, trying out the techniques on a straight, somewhat deserted stretch of road I cover most mornings. It adds variety and intensity to my daily workouts without requiring the full commitment and athletic ability required for the sport.

Race walking may become more popular in this country over the next few years, if its growing followings in Mexico, Japan, and many other countries are any indication. There are already more than one thousand competitive race walkers in the United States and another ten thousand who practice it non-competitively.

## 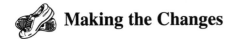 Making the Changes

With minor adjustments to your technique you can feel big differences in your walking from the very beginning. Try the bent-arm swing to feel an immediate difference in speed and intensity. Walk with straighter posture to get instant physical feedback that you are walking more smoothly. To see your stride lengthen on the spot, keep your steps as close as possible to a straight line.

These adjustments are simple compared to mastering the mechanics of a golf swing, a tennis serve, or a soccer kick. This is easy stuff! Still, many walkers do not bother even with these minor changes, choosing just to keep walking as they have always walked. They can get good exercise this way, but they will stay far below their potential. A willingness to make small adjustments can enhance the joy of living in many respects, and nowhere is this more true than in walking for fitness.

*"See, I am doing a new thing."*

*—Isaiah 43:19*

The saying "practice makes perfect" is absolutely true where changes to walking habits are concerned. The changes may feel strange at first, but they are easy to make, and they quickly begin to feel completely natural. You do not have to master new techniques to enjoy the benefits of fitness walking, but working on them will help you get the most out of your exercise. The key is to *get started.* Then you can experiment with some new twists on your lifetime walking techniques, reaping big fitness and health dividends.

*Chapter Ten*

# Your Personal Walking Program

*"A prudent man gives thought to his steps."*
*—Proverbs 14:15*

The way to begin walking for fitness simply is *to walk.* It does not matter how far or how fast. Just walk. When you take these first steps, you begin to get the most out of your effort.

Taking these vital first steps is really the secret of success, because you are actually *doing* something. Almost everyone who is overweight or out of shape intends to do something about it, but good intentions do not get the job done. Acting on good intentions does. As the familiar Nike shoe commercial says, "Just Do It!"

If you are serious about walking for fitness, you must get out of your easy chair and begin walking. If you have not already done this, put this book down right now and take a fifteen-minute stroll. Then pick the book up again and start building a comfortable, achievable plan for fitness walking—tailored just for you.

## Building a Walking Program

Developing a personal walking "program" may seem formal and unnecessary, but it is well worth the effort. A written plan for reaching your specific fitness goals gives structure that can make the difference between aimless wandering and dramatic, lasting impacts. It provides a road map to lead you from your current fitness status to better health and more vigorous living.

You could just follow a generic plan, but why should you when a personalized plan is so easy to build? You will control whether you follow through with a fitness program, so it makes sense to also control what this program will involve. There is a reason that custom-tailored clothing fits better than off-the-shelf varieties, and the same is true for fitness programs. Staying within basic guidelines, you can put together a personal walking program that is achievable, measurable, and—because it is tailored just for you—much more likely to be lasting and successful.

There are two basic landmarks on your walking program's road map: where you are and where you want to be. Everything else should help lead from the first to the second, but the route should be sensible. Trying to reach your goal too fast can be counterproductive and virtually assures failure. You cannot expect to lose twenty pounds in a week, and you cannot expect to go from being sedentary to race walking in that amount of time. Success with fitness walking is a matter of steps. A good personal walking program lays out these steps in a realistic and achievable pathway.

Most healthy people can measurably improve their cardiovascular fitness in just twelve weeks with a sensible, goal-based walking program. The goals will differ for each person. Some may simply want to shave a minute or so off their current time for walking a mile, while others may cut five or six minutes per mile from their beginning time. But for almost everyone there should be three basic goals: an increase in overall *distance,* an increase in the amount of *time spent walking,* and an increase in *speed.*

Since your goals are personal, they will depend on many factors—your age, your beginning physical condition, and the time available for exercise, to name a few. Unless you have unique physical problems, however, twelve weeks should be enough for you to see marked improvements in speed, distance, and duration. Before venturing onto the walking path, set goals for all three areas and make concrete plans for how to reach them.

 ## Setting Goals

Goals are an integral part of life. Whether formal or not, we all have goals from the time of our first conscious thoughts. Goals focus our energy and create pathways from dreams to reality.

In fitness walking as in so many other aspects of life, we begin with a vision of something we want to achieve. This vision may be better health, a slimmer body, or some other exercise benefit; but the vision alone will not get the job done. Goals are the bridge between the vision and its realization.

Successful business leaders have long understood the importance of goal-setting. Many consider corporate goals so important that they hang framed copies throughout their stores, factories, and offices as constant reminders to every employee.

Most of us are not this specific about our personal goals, but we should be. If we visualize what we want for the future and then chart step-by-step goals for achieving this vision, we can build better, richer lives. This is true in finance, relationships, spiritual development, and—for the matter at hand—in building health and fitness. Precise goals light the pathway to whatever we hope to be or attain, and they are surprisingly easy to develop if we follow some basic guidelines.

## *Our Goals Must Be Reasonable and Attainable*

Goals should make us stretch but also be realistic; they should not be impossible to reach. A sure way to stay frustrated is to make a goal unattainable, and a sure way to kill motivation is to make a goal too easy. A seventy-year-old diabetic should not expect to race walk at seven minutes per mile, and a healthy twenty-year-old should not expect to be satisfied with strolling along on twenty-minute miles. Goals that are either too easy or unrealistic are equally worthless.

For several years I directed annual multi-million-dollar charity drives in one of America's largest cities. Goal-setting was one of the most difficult parts of each year's fund-raising campaign. Some of our steering committee members always wanted to set the goal high enough to be just out of reach, thinking that unreachable goals would motivate people to keep striving and giving. Others fervently argued for goals that would be easy to reach, wanting to be sure everyone could enjoy the satisfaction of success regardless of their effort. Both views missed the mark.

Most of us have seen the cartoon where a mule keeps going forward because someone is holding a carrot out in front on a long stick. The mule never gets the carrot because the stick moves forward right along with him. He may keep going for a while, but even a mule will quit after enough of this. Chasing an unattainable goal is not motivating, and it dooms almost any effort to failure. On the other hand, the mule would probably not move at all if he could reach the carrot without any effort. To motivate, goals must be challenging but attainable.

Think about what you really want to accomplish with your walking. Do you hope to lose weight? Is there some specific disease or medical condition you hope to avoid or improve? Are you looking for a way to lower your cholesterol level or blood pressure? Do you simply want to get in better physical shape to feel better? From a physical standpoint, why are you beginning to walk?

These questions may be easy to answer in general terms, but real success calls for translating the generalities into specific numbers. For example, setting a goal to lose weight should include a specific number. The same is true for lowering cholesterol or blood-pressure levels. Even if the goal is simply to improve your physical condition, feel better, and work toward better overall health, there are still numbers to think about.

Numbers can be assigned to most fitness walking goals—especially distance, intensity, and duration. These are the basics: how far; how fast; and how long we want to walk. We can tailor all three to our individual needs, and we can express all three in specific numbers—concrete goals that are reasonable, attainable, and measurable.

## Our Goals Must Be Measurable

In an effort to keep up with tough international competition, American industry has increasingly turned to statistical controls. In a nutshell, this involves dividing every process into measurable parts—from manufacturing to sales to customer service. By keeping track of the numbers, it is easier to identify and fix any problem areas. Japanese companies began using statistical controls in a big way decades ago, and this played a large part in changing the image of "Made in Japan" from low-quality to high-quality products. America has followed suit, adopting many of the "Total Quality Management" principles that W. Edwards Deming—an American statistician and management consultant—used in helping Japan revitalize its industry in the years following World War II.

Statistical controls are as important to the success of a walking program as to a business plan. The chances for success in either increase significantly when specific numbers are used to (1) establish a starting point, (2) set reasonable but challenging goals, and then (3) track each step of progress along the way.

If this seems too dry and businesslike for a recreational activity, try it anyway. You will find it is a great source of motivation when you begin to see your progress in concrete terms. Nothing is more motivating in a weight-loss program than actually getting on the scales and seeing a lower number than the time before, or checking a measuring tape and finding that an unwanted inch has disappeared. Keeping track of miles and minutes can be just as motivating for a fitness walker. Tracking increases in distance, speed, and duration gives definition to our efforts in a way nothing else can. Also consider tracking a decrease in your resting heart rate. As you watch this number decrease, you will know that your heart is working more efficiently, pumping blood through your body in fewer beats. Goals motivate, and keeping track of our progress toward them encourages us to continue going forward.

Consider distance for example. It is amazing how quickly the miles add up when you walk regularly. If you walk three miles a day, seven days a week, and do not miss a day, you will cover 1,095 miles in a year—roughly the distance between Washington and Kansas City. Many walkers find it exciting to watch their mileage steadily mount, especially when they stop to realize how each mile brings better health and fitness.

If you are after success, why not use the same principles used by our most successful industries? After all, getting fit meets the criteria of a management process: identify a need (weight loss, better health, etc.); establish goals (weight, distance, blood pressure level, etc.); expend resources (time, energy, etc.); and hope for a profit (better, healthier living). Without measurable goals you will never know whether you have attained what you set out to achieve. Health and fitness are too important for a hit-or-miss approach. They deserve what any manager would use to achieve high priority results: attainable, measurable goals.

##  Taking Stock

Before setting goals for where you want to go, it is a good idea to know where you already are. This is true whether planning a trip, setting up a new business, or starting a walking program. If you are already in great physical shape, it makes no sense to begin with slow, short strolls. Conversely, if you have neglected exercise for a long time, you should not begin by trying to push the upper end of the aerobic walking range. No road map can help you have a smooth trip if you do not know your starting point.

When it comes to fitness—particularly aerobic fitness—it is good to start by pinpointing your current cardiovascular condition. If the basic objective is to get your heart and lungs working at their best, it makes sense to know how well they are already working. There are several methods for testing cardiovascular fitness. Some are administered by doctors or exercise specialists, but you can easily do others on your own.

One of the simplest and best self-tests is to simply time how long it takes you to walk one mile and compare the result to a cardiovascular fitness chart. It takes only a few minutes, and it requires no special equipment. You can do this test yourself on an athletic track, your neighborhood sidewalks, or any other smooth, level surface.

To prepare for taking a one-mile test, be sure the route you plan to walk is precisely one mile long. If you use a track at a school or athletic center, the distance should already be measured and marked. If you plan to use local streets or sidewalks, drive around your route in an automobile and use the car's odometer to measure exactly one mile. Get the starting and ending landmarks for this distance firmly fixed, then you will be ready to go.

With the route chosen and measured, simply walk a mile as fast as you can without becoming uncomfortable, keeping track of how long it takes. Do not run and do not push yourself too hard, but walk briskly instead of just strolling. Then write your time on the chart below. Repeat this process one day later to be sure you have an accurate appraisal and not a one-time anomaly, good or bad. Dr. William E. Oddon, developer of the Staywell Program, put together the following chart to quickly evaluate cardiovascular fitness. By comparing the times of your two test walks with Dr. Oddon's chart, you can get a fairly accurate appraisal of your current condition.

## <u>Step One:</u> *Find Your Cardiovascular Fitness Rating*

|  | Men | | Women | |
|---|---|---|---|---|
|  | <u>Under 40</u> | <u>Over 40</u> | <u>Under 40</u> | <u>Over 40</u> |
| Excellent: | 13:00 or less | 14:00 or less | 13:30 or less | 14:30 or less |
| Good: | 13:01–15:30 | 14:01–16:30 | 13:31–16:00 | 14:31–17:00 |
| Average: | 15:31–18:00 | 16:31–19:00 | 16:01–18:30 | 17:01–19:30 |
| Below Avg: | 18:01–19:30 | 19:01–21:30 | 18:30–20:00 | 19:31–22:00 |
| Low: | 19:31 or more | 21:31 or more | 20:01 or more | 22:01 or more |

**CHART NO. 3: CARDIOVASCULAR FITNESS RATING SCALE**

*First test:*

Date: _____    Minutes per mile: _____

Cardiovascular rating (circle one):

EXCELLENT    GOOD    AVERAGE    BELOW AVERAGE    LOW

## *Second test:*

Date: _____ Minutes per mile: _____

Cardiovascular rating (circle one):

EXCELLENT    GOOD    AVERAGE    BELOW AVERAGE    LOW

If you tested in the "excellent" range, you might be tempted to think that walking will not be challenging enough to help you meet your exercise goals. Think again. One of the great advantages of walking is that you can do it at any speed or intensity. If you are already streaking along at an impressive speed, you can focus on increasing your distance and duration. You can even push for greater speed, since top race walkers blaze along at less than seven minutes per mile. There is plenty of challenge here for everyone, from ardent athletes to couch potatoes. Anyone, regardless of age or physical condition, can set measurable, attainable walking goals that lead to better fitness.

## <u>Step 2:</u> *Set Your Personal Goals*

Your self test, using Dr. Oddon's chart, gave you a cardiovascular starting point. But there are other important considerations in goal setting. Only you can know what you really want to accomplish. Think about it and use the following blanks to help you visualize your definitive goals.

<u>Weight Goal</u>
Walking can play an important part in weight loss, but there are other factors involved such as diet. If you want to lose weight, set up a weight-control program that includes diet as well as exercise. To watch its effectiveness week-to-week, enter your current weight and what you want to weigh twelve weeks from today.

*Current Weight* _____    *Weight Goal* _____

## Speed Goal

The time it takes to walk a mile is a good indicator of cardiovascular fitness, and Dr. Oddon's chart makes it easy to see. If you scored less than "excellent" on the cardiovascular self test, you will probably want to set a goal of moving up to the "excellent" category. Jot down your current time as determined by your one-mile test walk, then record the time in which you would like to be walking a mile twelve weeks from today.

*Current: _____ min. per mile     Goal: _____ min. per mile*

## Distance Goal

This part may seem easier to accomplish than the two above, but it is not. In dealing with weight and speed, you can turn to specific numbers generated by a scale or a stopwatch. To come up with distance, you must do a bit of personal soul-searching.

If you are just beginning to walk for fitness, your current distance—how far you regularly walk—will probably be zero. You may be able to walk a fair distance, but *do* you? Also, how willing will you be to allot the time necessary for walking several miles at a time, several days each week? Some people are quite willing to spend forty-five minutes, an hour, or even more on their walking every day, but many others are not. Walking takes less time than many other exercises, but it does take time, so be realistic in deciding how much time you are willing to devote as you set your distance goals.

The numbers you put in these two blanks should be the number of miles you walk now and the number of miles you want to be walking in twelve weeks, when your exercise routine is fully up to speed. A good way to find this second number is to take the speed goal you just established and divide it into the amount of time you plan to spend on each walk. This will give you a good distance goal, though you may find you want to refine it a bit after looking over some of the sample programs shown later in this chapter.

*Current: _____ miles each walk     Goal: _____ miles each walk*

## Duration Goal

How long you plan to walk during each exercise session is a matter of personal choice. It primarily depends on how much time and energy you are willing to devote to exercise. For some, this may be only fifteen- to twenty minutes per day, while others will devote an hour or more. One great advantage of walking is that it is effective whether the doses are large or small.

A key consideration should be when and how you plan to do your walking. If you plan to walk in early morning or late evening, your time may not be as constrained as if you walk during a business lunch hour. This is one reason I prefer walking early in the morning. It allows me to have the exercise behind me before I shower and prepare for my day, eliminating the need for exercise and cleanup time after I am into my work routine. Many have told me they cannot exercise at this hour, however, some saying they need the lift that exercise provides in the middle of their business day. It is a personal choice, but how much time you have enters into the "duration" part of your goal setting.

For really good results, you should try to walk at least thirty minutes per session. Aerobic conditioning requires raising your heartbeat into the aerobic training range and keeping it there for at least twenty minutes. It is hard to do this consistently with less than half-hour exercise sessions.

Walking about forty-five minutes per session is ideal. This gives ample time to warm up, push the heartbeat into the aerobic range, and then cool down again before quitting. After a twelve-week starter program, most people can easily walk at least three miles in forty-five minutes, a level that produces high payoff in aerobic conditioning and calorie burning. For long-term fitness and weight control, your duration goal should be somewhere in the forty-five minute range. More important, though, it should be the amount of time you will honestly, regularly commit to your walking.

*Current: _____ minutes per walk     Goal: _____ minutes per walk*

## Frequency Goal

Frequency, like distance and duration, is a matter of personal choice. Some experts say we should exercise every day, while others say an occasional day of rest is beneficial. Most agree, though, that aerobic exercise requires keeping the heart beating in its aerobic training range for at least twenty minutes at least three times a week. This should be the minimum.

A good goal for fitness walking is five sessions per week. Essentially this means planning to walk every day but allowing for the occasional day when your weather, schedule, or mood simply makes exercising impractical. Walking every day produces the best results, but it is often hard to do. Setting a goal of five times per week accomplishes almost the same thing, but it avoids a set up for failure.

*Current: _____ walks per week     Goal: _____ walks per week*

 **Your Starting Point**

You've set your goals; now where should you start? The answer is not the same for everyone. If you are already very active physically, you may want to begin at the speed clocked in your one-mile test and then focus on building greater distance and duration over the first twelve weeks. If you have been sedentary for a long time, though, you might do better to drop back from your test speed and begin at a slower pace. After all, the test mile was to see how fast you can walk now. Just because you *can* walk this fast once does not mean you *should* walk this fast—at least not yet.

To decide your starting speed, go out and take another test walk. This time just walk a quarter of a mile, and do not force yourself to walk as fast as you did before. Instead, walk at a comfortable but aggressive pace. You do not want to start by slowly strolling if you can do much better, but neither should you overexert yourself in the beginning. Multiply the results of your quarter-mile walk by four, and enter the result. This is your beginning speed.

*Beginning Speed:* _____

 **Intermediate Steps**

It is easy to identify your starting points and ultimate goals. It is trickier to develop intermediate steps that can sensibly lead from the first of these landmarks to the second. You do not want to build up your walking speed and duration so fast that it overtaxes your body, but neither do you want to take it so easy that you become bored.

In designing a twelve-week starter program, it is good to plan to gradually increase your speed, distance, and duration. If you take the differences between your starting and goal figures and divide them into eight increments, you get good, weekly intermediate goals.

Week 1: Walk at the beginning pace.
Week 2: Increase by one-eighth of the total goal.
Week 3: Increase by one-eighth of the total goal.
Week 4: Level off and maintain the Week 3 pace.
Week 5: Increase by one-eighth of the total goal.
Week 6: Increase by one-eighth of the total goal.
Week 7: Level off and maintain the Week 6 pace.

Week 8: Increase by one-eighth of the total goal.
Week 9: Increase by one-eighth of the total goal.
Week 10: Level off and maintain the Week 9 pace.
Week 11: Increase by one-eighth of the total goal.
Week 12: Increase by one-eighth of the total goal.

Notice that every third week contains no planned increases. These leveling-off weeks allow you to become comfortable with your gains—and comfort is a key factor in walking. You could probably build up your speed and duration more quickly, but it might leave you more fatigued and discouraged than you want to be. A good exercise program should be something to anticipate happily, not something to dread. A slow, sensible buildup ensures this.

Speed, distance, and duration will all pick up quite naturally over the weeks, but it may be tempting to push ahead more quickly. Resist this temptation. The body needs time to adjust along the way, so do not try to do too much too fast. If you do you may find yourself tiring too quickly, feeling exhausted instead of invigorated, and becoming reluctant to continue.

The numbers in your goals may not fit perfectly with the eight-increment formula, so use some sensible latitude in building your chart. The main thing to remember is that increases in speed, distance, and duration should all be phased in slowly and simultaneously. You may want to add three minutes per week to your walks over the entire twelve weeks, for example, increasing the duration by thirty-six minutes. Or you may want to steadily add to your mileage in quarter-mile increments.

As the fable about the tortoise and the hare teaches us, "Slow and steady wins the race." Moving toward your goals in bite-size increments is easy on the body, yet it produces enormous results in just twelve weeks. This race is to good health, and a comfortable, sensible pace is the best way to be sure you win this worthwhile prize.

## Your Personal Walking Program

The data you have developed by using the last few pages will be the foundation for your personal walking program. All you have to do is put it all together. The following chart has spaces for you to enter your starting points, your goals, and your weekly increments that will lead from one to the other. Fill in the blanks, and you will have a walking program tailored especially for you.

Before you build your personal program, you may want to look at some sample programs that have been built for others of varied ages, goals, and physical situations.

# Example Walking Program: An Average Healthy Person

This program was built for a healthy man in his late forties, but it could easily be used by most healthy women as well as men. Although not a regular exerciser, this man wanted to begin working on his overall fitness with a regular walking program. After testing in the "good" category on the self-test of cardiovascular health, he set a goal to be in the "excellent" category within three months.

This program steadily increased his walking time over the twelve weeks, from twelve minutes up to forty-two minutes per walk. At the same time, it steadily increased his speed from an easy twenty-four minutes per mile starting pace down to an energetic fourteen minutes per mile. His distance increased, too, from a half mile at the start to three miles after twelve weeks.

This is a good, sensible program for any individual who is basically healthy. It gets the new walker into the "excellent" cardiovascular category while leaving room for still more increases in speed, distance, and duration.

## Walking Program for Person in Average Condition

| Week | (miles) Distance | (minutes spent walking) Duration | (times per week) Frequency |
|------|------------------|----------------------------------|----------------------------|
| 1 | .5 | 12 | 3–4 |
| 2 | .75 | 15 | 3–4 |
| 3 | 1.0 | 18 | 3–4 |
| 4 | 1.25 | 21 | 3–4 |
| 5 | 1.5 | 24 | 4–5 |
| 6 | 1.5 | 24 | 4–5 |
| 7 | 1.75 | 27 | 4–5 |
| 8 | 2.0 | 30 | 4–5 |
| 9 | 2.25 | 33 | 5–6 |
| 10 | 2.5 | 36 | 5–6 |
| 11 | 2.75 | 39 | 5–6 |
| 12 | 3.0 | 42 | 5–6 |

# Example Walking Program: A Physically Active Person

This plan was built for a person who was already in excellent physical condition. He was turning to walking because of joint problems that were beginning to result from high-impact exercising. He scored in the "excellent" range on the cardiovascular health self-test, and his goal was to build time and speed over the twelve weeks. An avid exerciser, he wanted to set the stage for later moving up to race-walking speeds.

Because his stamina had already been built through other exercising, this walker began by going greater distances at a much faster pace than the walker in the first example. Two miles per walk at fifteen minutes per mile was a sensible, easy beginning for this walker, yet a walking goal of four twelve-minute miles presented all the challenge he could want.

## Walking Program for Physically Active Person

| | (miles) | (minutes spent walking) | (times per week) |
|---|---|---|---|
| **Week** | **Distance** | **Duration** | **Frequency** |
| 1 | 2.0 | 30 | 3–4 |
| 2 | 2.25 | 30 | 3–4 |
| 3 | 2.5 | 35 | 3–4 |
| 4 | 2.75 | 35 | 3–4 |
| 5 | 2.75 | 35 | 4–5 |
| 6 | 3.0 | 40 | 4–5 |
| 7 | 3.0 | 40 | 4–5 |
| 8 | 3.25 | 40 | 4–5 |
| 9 | 3.5 | 45 | 5–6 |
| 10 | 3.5 | 45 | 5–6 |
| 11 | 3.75 | 45 | 5–6 |
| 12 | 4.0 | 48 | 5–6 |

## Example Walking Program: An Older or Inactive Person

This program was built for a senior citizen who had some health problems. After being relatively inactive for many years, she wanted to improve her health by walking. She had no intention of ever walking at high speeds, but she was anxious to build greater heart and lung capacity.

Her program began gently, adding distance and duration but never increasing speed. It took her from a sedentary lifestyle to the capability of exercising for forty minutes almost every day. This was a major jump, and it offered enormous health benefits. Using the foundation built during this kind of twelve-week starter program, most senior adults could slowly increase their speed and distance in lifelong programs of fitness walking.

## Walking Program for Older or Physically Inactive Person

|  | (miles) | (minutes spent walking) | (times per week) |
|---|---|---|---|
| **Week** | **Distance** | **Duration** | **Frequency** |
| 1 | 0 .5 | 10 | 3–4 |
| 2 | 0.75 | 15 | 3–4 |
| 3 | 0 .75 | 15 | 3–4 |
| 4 | 1.0 | 20 | 3–4 |
| 5 | 1.0 | 20 | 4–5 |
| 6 | 1.25 | 25 | 4–5 |
| 7 | 1.25 | 25 | 4–5 |
| 8 | 1.5 | 30 | 4–5 |
| 9 | 1.5 | 30 | 5–6 |
| 10 | 1.75 | 35 | 5–6 |
| 11 | 1.75 | 35 | 5–6 |
| 12 | 2.0 | 40 | 5–6 |

## Check with the Doc!

As you should do before beginning any exercise program, check with your doctor before getting started with fitness walking. I include this statement for obvious legal liability reasons, but also because it makes sense. Walking poses fewer risks than just about any other form of exercise, but your health is too important to leave even the slightest doubt. In very few circumstances will a doctor advise against fitness walking, but it is still a very good idea to ask.

 ## To Chart or Not to Chart

Do you really need to chart a formal walking program before beginning? This depends on whether you want to get the most out of the time you plan to invest in fitness.

All major investments deserve careful planning. Thousands of small businesses fail each year because their owners do not take the time to build solid business plans before opening their doors. Major corporations spend months, even years, on planning every angle—research to manufacturing to marketing—before launching new product lines. Even big personal investments such as new homes and automobiles generally involve a significant amount of planning in most families.

Fitness takes a big investment of time. If you are serious about it, you should expect to devote several hours to it each week for the rest of your life. This is a lot of time! If you start by just stepping out your door and walking, this shortchanges your investment. Knowing how fast, how far, and how long you need to walk can help you get bigger dividends from the time you invest. If you expect results, spend a little time on the planning that can help you meet your expectations.

There is nothing magic about filling out a planning chart. The magic is in what following a well designed exercise plan can produce. Step-by-step, week-by-week, it can lead you from your starting point to sensible goals without either overtaxing your body or letting it go unchallenged. It only takes a few minutes to build the plan for your first twelve weeks of exercise. Invest these few more minutes now, and reap the benefits.

The following chart will lead you to your personal fitness walking program.

# Personal Walking Program for

_____

|      | (miles) | (minutes spent walking) | (times per week) |
|:----:|:-------:|:-----------------------:|:----------------:|
| **Week** | **Distance** | **Duration** | **Frequency** |
| 1    | 3–4     |                         |                  |
| 2    | 3–4     |                         |                  |
| 3    | 3–4     |                         |                  |
| 4    | 3–4     |                         |                  |
| 5    | 4–5     |                         |                  |
| 6    | 4–5     |                         |                  |
| 7    | 4–5     |                         |                  |
| 8    | 4–5     |                         |                  |
| 9    | 5–6     |                         |                  |
| 10   | 5–6     |                         |                  |
| 11   | 5–6     |                         |                  |
| 12   | 5–6     |                         |                  |

Now you have a plan. Get up, get out, go for it—and ask the Lord to walk with you!

*Chapter Eleven*

# Your Daily Walks

*"Whoever claims to live in him must walk as Jesus did."*
*—1 John 2:6*

Good intentions, well conceived goals, even sensible exercise plans—all are worthless without action. The enormous physical and spiritual benefits of walking are found on the pathway, not on paper. With your plans complete for when, where, how, and how long to walk, the next step is to begin.

A good session of walking, like a good book or speech, should have three main parts: a good beginning; a good middle; and a good end. This may sound simplistic, but people abandon exercise programs every day because they ignore one or more of these parts. Many who are just starting out want to skip the beginning and go straight to an aerobic training pace. By not bothering to properly warm up before their exercise or cool down properly afterward, they experience soreness or injury instead of an exercise afterglow. Paying attention to all three parts can keep invigorating exercise from turning into a painful experience.

Can an exercise as simple as walking really be done so incorrectly that it is painful? Absolutely! Without warm-up exercises to increase circulation and flexibility, walking can—and often does—result in sore muscles. The same result can come from ending a walking session too abruptly after reaching a strong aerobic pace. One of the great advantages of walking for exercise is its lack of stress on muscles and joints, and this is too good an advantage to throw away by skipping the warm-up and cool-down steps to save a couple of minutes.

According to an old adage, we never have enough time to do something right, but we always have enough time to do it over. Walking should be an exception. If we take the time to do our exercising right the first time, we can make it more pleasant and more effective. We can also prevent unwanted and potentially damaging side effects. This is why it makes such good sense to *plan* our exercise sessions instead of just let them happen. The planning is quick and easy, and ensures that we get the most out of the valuable time we invest in fitness.

##  Warming Up

Warming up for a fitness walk takes only about five minutes, but it does great things for your body. Think of warm-up exercises as a series of stepping stones, leading from your normal activity level to the accelerated pace of aerobic exercise. The exercises stretch your muscles, loosen your joints, expand your lungs, increase your heart rate, and effectively shift your entire body into a higher gear. This helps every-thing operate more efficiently— from muscles to the cardiovascular system. You can walk without warming up, but you will greatly increase your risk of sprains, strains, and pains if you do.

The easiest way to warm up for walking fast is to first walk slowly. Instead of just taking off at full speed, start with a stroll and then gradually pick up the pace. As you do, your blood will start flowing at a faster rate, the temperature of your muscles and tendons will rise, and your joints will begin loosening. After two or three minutes you will be ready to stop for a few brief stretching exercises. Many walkers and joggers do their stretching exercises cold, but the muscles respond better after being loosened by two or three minutes of walking.

Stretching is preventative maintenance for the body. When I fly, I would rather have a ground crew spend extra time getting the airplane ready before take-off than risk having problems develop in the air, even if it means a slight delay. The same principle applies to stretching. It lets us prevent problems and pain by paying proper attention to our basic equipment. Stretching lengthens our muscles, increases our muscle flexibility, and keeps our range of motion free in all the joints we use in walking. A few minutes of stretching prior to take-off can ensure that each walk is a pleasant, trouble-free trip.

No walking experts are likely to dispute the importance of stretching, but do not expect any two to agree precisely which exercises are best. Some recommend using six or eight stretching exercises, while others suggest only two or three. Whatever the number, or whatever the specific exercises might be, the key is to stretch the muscles that will get the greatest workout in walking. This way the vital muscles are warmed up before they are heavily exercised, and are less likely to cause problems and pain. The following exercises will do this job quite nicely.

## Wall Stand

The "wall stand" stretches the calf muscles at the back of your lower legs and the Achilles tendons at the back of your heels. Simply face a tree or wall, standing two or three feet away, and lean forward with your arms straightened at about shoulder height. Keep your toes pointed forward and your heels flat on the ground as you bend your arms at the elbow, leaning forward a bit more. You will feel the muscles stretching in your heels and calves. Hold this position for about fifteen seconds, then stand up straight again. Repeat several times.

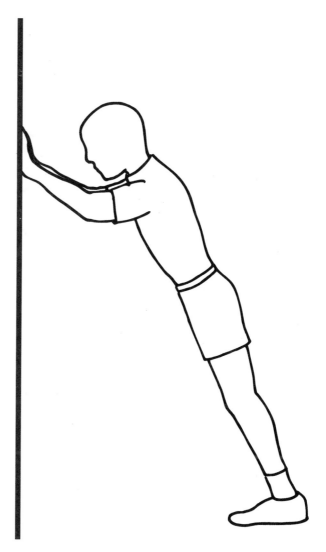

## Quadriceps and Knee Stretch

This exercise stretches the big muscles on the front of your thighs and the tendons that bridge the kneecaps to connect the upper and lower parts of your legs. Use a tree or wall again—this time for balance. Stand on your left foot and, with your right hand flat against the tree or wall, reach back with your left hand to grab your right ankle. Keeping your back straight, pull this foot back until your knee is pointing to the ground. When you feel the muscles stretching down the front of your thigh and across the knee, hold this position for about fifteen seconds. Then switch to the other foot and do the same thing. Repeat the process several times.

## *Hamstring Stretch*

This exercise stretches the hamstrings, those large tendons that attach to the back of your knees and run up to your pelvis.

Sit with your legs stretched out in front of you. Slowly reach for your feet. Hold this stretch for about fifteen seconds, then straighten your torso before repeating the stretch.

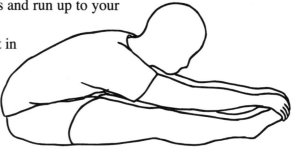

 **Upper Body Stretches**

Don't neglect to stretch the muscles in your upper body, as well. Try these stretches the next time you walk:

- Lace your fingers together in front of you and push your palms out and away from you. You should feel the stretch in your arms and across your shoulders.

- Now link your fingers behind your back and gently pull your arms up to stretch your chest muscles.

• Stretch your triceps, the muscles in back of your upper arm, by putting your arm over your head, and bending your arm at the elbow. Your elbow should be pointing straight up while your hand rests on your back. Hold the stretch with your opposite hand on your elbow. Repeat with opposite arm.

• Now with one hand on your waist, slowly bend to the side with your opposite arm overhead. Repeat, bending in other direction. This will stretch your waist and the muscles in your side and back.

# A Cardiovascular Workout

The main course of your walking session is the cardiovascular workout. This is aerobic exercise, the kind that produces big health benefits. Obviously it deserves the majority of your walking time, and you should plan to walk fast enough and long enough to keep your heartbeat in the "aerobic training range" for at least twenty minutes.

## Aerobic Exercise

To qualify as aerobic exercise, an activity must be strenuous enough to get your heart beating at between 60-85 percent of its predicted maximum rate—your "aerobic training range." This takes vigorous activity, and it must be sustained for at least twenty consecutive minutes to really be helpful. Exercise at this rate at least three times a week, and you will get the full benefits of aerobic exercise.

Your aerobic training range depends on your age, and how fast you reach it depends on your physical condition. If you start out in poor physical condition, it may take very little strenuous walking to get your heart pumping at 60-85 percent of its predicted maximum rate. After several weeks of exercise, though, you should find yourself having to work harder to get your heart pumping at this level. This is what you want, because it is clear evidence that your heart and lungs are getting stronger.

It is easy to determine your own aerobic training range. First, find your predicted maximum heart rate (PMHR) by subtracting your age from 220. Sixty percent of this number is the bottom end of your aerobic training range and 85 percent is the top end. By working the following three math problems—approximately fifth-grade level—you can find your own aerobic training range.

 # Finding Your Aerobic Training Range

Step 1: Subtract your age from 220.

$$220 - \underline{\phantom{xxxx}} = \underline{\phantom{xxxx}}$$
$$\quad\quad\;\; \text{(age)} \quad\; \text{(PMHR)}$$

*Step 2:* Multiply your PMHR (Predicted Maximum Heart Rate) by 60 percent to get the low end of range.

_____ x .60 = _____
(PMHR)      (low end)

*Step 3:* Multiply your PMHR (Predicted Maximum Heart Rate) by 85 percent to get the top end of range.

_____ x .85 = _____
(PMHR)      (high end)

*Step 4:* Your personal aerobic training range is from

_____ to _____ heart beats per minute.
(from Step 2)  (from Step 3)

## Aerobic Training Ranges (by Age)

The aerobic training range drops with age, so a fifty-year-old does not have to exercise as strenuously as a thirty-year-old to get aerobic training benefits. This is one reason why walking is ideal for all ages. A well conditioned twenty-year-old can get an exhausting physical challenge and reap great aerobic benefits through strenuous race walking. Then, twenty-five years later, the same aerobic training benefits are still available through walking at a slower but still demanding thirteen-minute-mile pace. Another twenty-five years can pass, and the aerobic exercise benefits can still accrue in less strenuous walking around a mall, a neighborhood, or any number of other safe, convenient places.

The average aerobic training range drops steadily with age.

## Aerobic Training Range by Age
(measured in heartbeats per minute)

| Age | PMHR | Training Range |
|-----|------|----------------|
| 20 | 200 | 120 – 170 |
| 25 | 195 | 117 – 166 |
| 30 | 190 | 114 – 162 |
| 35 | 185 | 111 – 157 |
| 40 | 180 | 108 – 153 |
| 45 | 175 | 105 – 149 |
| 50 | 170 | 102 – 145 |
| 55 | 165 | 99 – 140 |
| 60 | 160 | 96 – 136 |
| 65 | 155 | 93 – 132 |
| 70 | 150 | 90 – 128 |
| 75 | 145 | 87 – 123 |

**CHART NO. 4: AEROBIC TRAINING HEART RATE**

## Finding and Keeping the Right Speed

The walking pace needed to get your heart beating in its aerobic training range may differ from the pace your spouse or good friend might need. The only way to find the right speed for yourself is to get out and walk, pausing at regular intervals to check your heartbeat. On-the-spot heart monitoring is the right way to accurately tell whether you are reaching your aerobic training pace.

After about five minutes of warm-up walking and stretching, increase your speed to a challenging but not uncomfortable pace. After about five minutes of walking at this speed, stop just long enough to take your pulse. If your heartbeat is in your aerobic training range, resume walking at this pace for the remainder of your session. If you are below your aerobic training range, pick up the pace, and then pause five minutes farther down the trail to take your pulse again. If your heartbeat is above the aerobic training range, do the opposite: Slow down a bit. After two or three checks, you should be walking at a comfortable rate with your heart pumping in its correct aerobic range.

Checking your pulse on the walking path only takes a few seconds, and it is easy to do. Simply find your pulse at your wrist or neck (see diagram below), and use a watch to check your pulse rate. You do not need to time your pulse for a whole minute; just count the number of beats in six seconds and add a zero. If the number you get is in your aerobic training range, you are set to go.

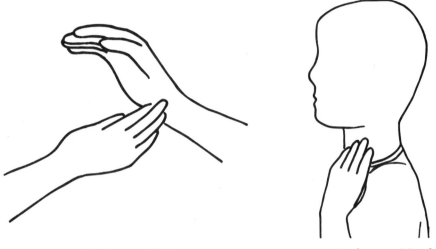

*Pulse at Wrist*          *Pulse at Neck*

Some walking tracks—particularly those built or sponsored by medical facilities—have begun installing special devices to help with pulse checks. These usually consist of small lights mounted on posts about every quarter mile along the trail. The lights automatically blink on and off at ten second intervals to help you time your pulse. If your track has this equipment, you can pause, find a good pulse point, and count the heartbeats between blinks of the light. Quickly multiplying the result by six gives you your pulse rate, and you are quickly on your way again. This is a wonderful innovation that should spread to more and more walking tracks and trails over the next few years.

 **Your Resting Pulse**

Checking your heart rate when you are *not* walking can reveal the impact your walking is having on your heart. You resting pulse should drop considerably several weeks after you begin exercising, as mine did. Before I began exercising, my resting heart rate was 78— just over the 75-beats-per-minute that is typical for an unfit

# Heart Rate Chart

Once each week, check your resting heart rate just before taking your fitness walk. Then stop about halfway through that day's walk to check your exercise heart rate.

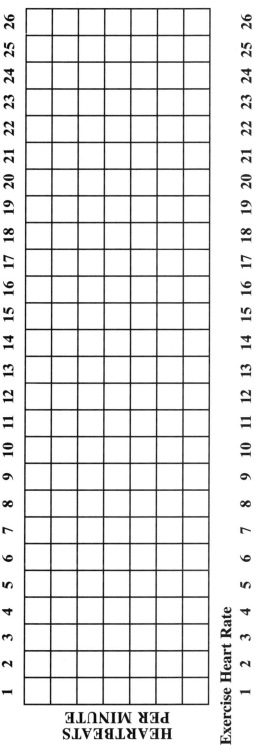

**Resting Heart Rate**

1  2  3  4  5  6  7  8  9  10  11  12  13  14  15  16  17  18  19  20  21  22  23  24  25  26

HEARTBEATS PER MINUTE

**Exercise Heart Rate**

1  2  3  4  5  6  7  8  9  10  11  12  13  14  15  16  17  18  19  20  21  22  23  24  25  26

HEARTBEATS PER MINUTE

**CHART NO. 5: HEART RATE CHART**

person. Now, twenty years older, I have a resting heart rate of 48—just under the 50-beats-per-minute considered typical for one who is physically fit.

## *Directions for Chart No. 5*

A good way to follow your progress on and off the track is by charting both your resting heart rate and the rate you reach when exercising. Your exercise heart rate should remain fairly constant as your walking speed increases over the first few months. Your resting heart rate, on the other hand, should take a significant dive—clear evidence that your heart muscle is getting stronger and healthier. Jotting down the numbers from week to week and watching the trend line head south is visible and motivating proof that your investment of time and energy is paying big health dividends. *See Chart No. 5 on page 137.*

 **Cooling Down**

If you watch racers—whether runners or race walkers—you will notice that they do not immediately stop when they cross the finish line. Instead they keep going gradually slowing their pace and cooling down. This cool-down period is critical for the racers, and it is just as important in your own workouts. In fact, it is even more important than the warm-up. Letting your body come down slowly from its accelerated activity level helps avoid some problems that can come with an abrupt stop.

During exercise, high levels of adrenaline can build up in your blood. The adrenaline is consumed during the intense exercise, but it can accumulate for a few minutes if intense activity suddenly stops. For a few especially sensitive people, these accumulations can pose a danger to the heart. Cooling down allows the chemicals that have built up to metabolize and lets their production taper off gradually.

To get a feel for the problem, imagine the difference between driving your car down a two-foot hill or into a two-foot pothole. Both would take you down to the same level, but the pothole would give your car a damaging shock while the gentle slope of a two-foot hill would feel smooth as silk. The same principle applies to cooling off after exercising. It helps cushion your body from the sudden drop in activity and lets your heart rate decrease to its resting state. Your muscles clear themselves of waste products, and your blood vessels constrict as the blood flow is gradually redirected. All of your body's systems that have felt the increased demands of exercise begin getting back to normal, and this takes a little time.

You should allow about five minutes for cooling down, and you can approach it in a couple of ways. Ideally you should walk for a few minutes, gradually slowing your pace, then spend time doing stretching exercises—the same ones you used to begin your session. When your heartbeat drops to less than one hundred beats per minute, it is usually safe to stop.

Taking a few minutes to cool down will end your session more safely, and it will also leave you feeling better. Your body may come down from its intensity, but your spirit will stay elevated. Millions say they do their best work in the hours just after exercising, and many find the cooling down minutes to be a perfect time to crystallize the thoughts they had while walking. Like a good novel, it wraps things up neatly and lets you go forth knowing you are not quite the same as when you started.

##  The Total Session

When you add up the three basic parts—warming up, aerobic training, and cooling down—you have a complete exercise session. Starting from a standstill, your minutes of warming and loosening up begin to raise your heart rate. Then this rate moves into the aerobic training range as you shift into high gear. After at least twenty minutes of good aerobic exercise you taper off and let your heart rate drop toward its resting rate.

Graphically displayed, the session should look something like the chart on page 141. The times may vary, depending on how much time you are willing to personally invest in each the three phases, but the curve should resemble the one on the chart.

The importance of warming up and cooling down becomes clearer when we recognize that walking is serious exercise. No one would think of running a twenty-six-mile marathon without using some exercises to loosen leg muscles and just generally warm-up. Nor would any marathoner stop cold after crossing the finish line several hours later. The potential for severe body damage is simply too obvious. In fitness walking the same principles apply. The potential damage may be neither as obvious nor as severe, but it can and does happen. If you construct your exercise sessions to include warming up and cooling down, you can keep it from happening to your own body.

If you are only going to stroll around the neighborhood, pausing to chat with friends and taking a gentle, hands-in-your-pockets pace, the warm-up and cool-down periods are not needed. If you want to use your walking time to truly build fitness, however, treat each session with the seriousness of a marathon runner. Construct each session like a good novel—with a strong beginning, a strong middle, and a strong end.

# Fitness Walking Session

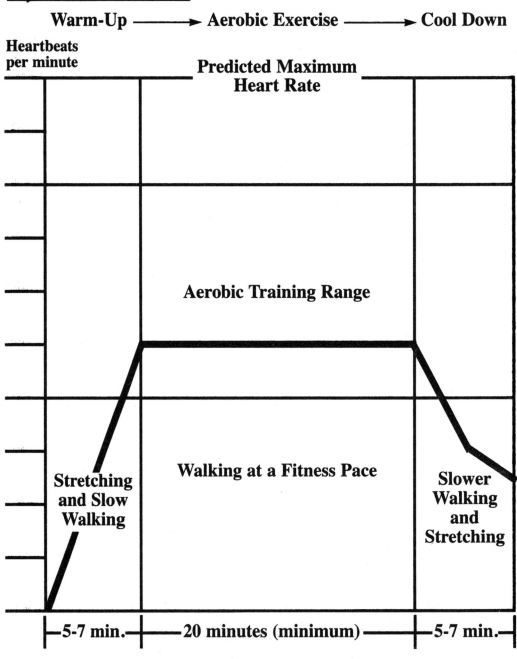

_Physical Exercise Phases_

**Warm-Up** ⟶ **Aerobic Exercise** ⟶ **Cool Down**

**Heartbeats per minute**

**Predicted Maximum Heart Rate**

**Aerobic Training Range**

**Stretching and Slow Walking**

**Walking at a Fitness Pace**

**Slower Walking and Stretching**

├─5-7 min.─┤├──20 minutes (minimum)──┤├─5-7 min.─┤

**CHART NO. 6: FITNESS WALKING SESSION**

## Strength Training

The maximum benefit from muscle training will come from consistent, supervised workouts at a reputable health club or training facility. But you can begin to get benefits on your own with simple exercises done with a pair of hand weights. Buy weights that are not so heavy you cannot lift them, but aren't so light that you do not have to work your muscles to lift them after several repetitions. When repeating an exercise, you should have difficulty completing the last repetitions. This "burn" is building the muscle and helping you get the most from the workout. If you continually finish an exercise with ease, try a heavier weight or add more repetitions.

Here are some suggested upper-body exercises. Do three sets of the following exercises, at least twice a week:

• **Biceps curls**—With one weight in each hand, stand with your elbows to your side and hands down in front of you, palms out. Slowly bring the weights toward your shoulders then lower them again, keeping your elbows in place. Repeat 10 times.

Now bring your arms to your side, with thumbs pointing forward. Curl the weights toward your shoulders, then bring it down again. Repeat 10 times.

• **Triceps curl**—With a weight in your right hand, put your hand behind your back with your elbow pointing toward the sky (same position as triceps stretch). Support the back of your right arm with your left hand. Slowly straighten your arm, lifting the weight toward the sky. Lower it to the original position. Repeat 10 times with each arm.

• **Upward press**—With a weight in each hand, stand with arms to the side bent to a 90-degree angle, shoulders and elbows at the same level. Press weights slowly above your head and lower to starting position. Repeat 10 times.

Now bring hands to your shoulders and press weights straight out in front of you. Repeat 10 times.

• **Straight arm lift**—With a weight in each hand and arms down by your side, slowly lift your arms straight out in front of you and back down. Repeat 10 times.

Look to other sources for more muscle training exercises that would be simple enough for you to do after your walk. Fitness magazines, websites, and professional trainers can give you ideas for strength training and toning. Vary your exercises to use each large muscle group of the body.

*Chapter Twelve*

# Stepping Off

*"Your word is a lamp to my feet and a light for my path."*
*—Psalm 119:105*

Habits, whether good or bad, naturally develop as we do things repeatedly over a long period of time. This has certainly been true for me in my walks with God. I have settled into a comfortable pattern for my walks, one that blends the spiritual aspects with the physical routine to ensure that I get the most out of both. Here is how the two work together:

| **Physical** | **Spiritual** |
|---|---|
| Warm up with slow walking and stretching. | Memorize the day's verse, and get the key points in mind. |

While using warm-up exercises to limber my muscles and increase the blood flow throughout my body, I lock the day's Scripture verse securely in my mind. I simply recite it to myself at the beginning of each warm-up exercise. Using the three basic exercises shown in Chapter 12, this means I review the verse three times—enough to secure it in my mind so that I will be able to think about it during my walk and long afterwards.

144

| Physical | Spiritual |
|---|---|
| Begin the walking pace. | Apply the verse personally. |

As I step off and begin my walk, I begin thinking about the verse I have memorized. If I need reminding, I pull out the card and review the verse. For several minutes I try to think about what the verse means to me personally. I do not dwell as much on the biblical context as I do on the words themselves, trying to connect them to my own life and needs—finding the guidance God might be giving me through this particular piece of Scripture.

| Physical | Spiritual |
|---|---|
| Reach full stride and speed. | Pray, starting with the theme of the Scripture verse. |

By the time I have reflected on the day's verse for several minutes, connecting it to my own life, I have reached full stride and am walking at a vigorous pace. This is when I begin praying. I usually start by talking to God about the verse on which I have focused. I may ask Him for greater understanding, to lift the veil and let me know what guidance it contains specifically for me. Or if it has really hit home regarding some problem, concern, weakness, or joy, I simply talk with my God about it. From this point on the prayer becomes a conversation, which usually lasts until I realize I have reached the end of my route for this day.

| Physical | Spiritual |
|---|---|
| Walk slower to cool down. | Plan how to act on the ideas, feelings, and concerns that have emerged while walking. |

After talking with God for a half hour or more, I usually have lots of ideas. Often in praying for others I emerge with items to add to my day's "to do" list—calls, notes, or visits to follow through. The variety of things I feel compelled to remember, do, or discuss with my wife or others after a walk seems endless. I use the time when I am physically cooling down to crystallize these ideas into concrete terms so I can quickly jot them down before hitting the shower.

These spiritual and physical exercise patterns are graphically merged on the following chart. The physical exercise plan is exactly as you will see it in Chapter 11, with a spiritual pattern overlaid. This chart illustrates how the basic elements of spiritual exercise (focus thought, extended reflection, prayer, and follow-up planning) fit with a sensible fitness walking routine.

# Fitness Walking Session

*Physical Exercise Phases*

**Warm-Up ———➤ Aerobic Exercise ———➤ Cool Down**

**Heartbeats
per minute**

**Predicted Maximum
Heart Rate**

**Aerobic Training Range**

**Walking at a Fitness Pace**

**Stretching
and Slow
Walking**

**Slower
Walking
and
Stretching**

⊢**5-7 min.**⊣⊢————**20 minutes (minimum)**————⊢**5-7 min.**⊣

*Spiritual Exercise Phases*

| Read and Memorize Walking Card Verse | ➤ | Apply Verse to Own Life | ➤ | Begin Praying About Theme of Walking Card Verse | ➤ | Prayer | ➤ | Praise | ➤ | Plan How to Act on Concerns and Ideas |

**CHART NO. 7: WALKING WITH GOD—TOTAL SESSION**

Charts and formulas tend to make things seem complex; however, walking alone with God is anything but. It is simple, but it is a bonding experience beyond measure. It is very personal time shared by Master and mortal. And it can be truly life-changing. Once you have made the connection, it is hard to imagine life ever being quite the same.

 ## The First Twelve Weeks

The journey to better physical and spiritual fitness begins with a single footstep. This may be a poor paraphrase of an old Chinese proverb, but it is true. If you filled in the blanks as you went along, you now have a plan—a personalized plan—that can take you to a better level of physical fitness. Armed with ideas about everything from aerobic heart rates to walking cards, your next logical step is to actually get started. All that remains is to take this first step.

From the physical fitness angle this just means putting on your walking shoes and taking the first step. From the spiritual fitness angle it means building your focus so that you turn every minute of your exercise time into walking with God.

For your first twelve weeks of walking, why not focus on a personal spiritual tune-up? Think about what you really believe, about your own faith, and about what it takes to live a Christian life—in short, think about your own walk with God.

Writing a Scripture verse on a file card and taking it on your walk can do wonders for keeping your focus on God. Refer back to chapter 5 for ideas on how to tailor walking cards to fit your own needs, then try using the following verses for the first twelve weeks. By the time you use the last of these, you should have achieved all the physical goals of your personal walking plan and a spiritual tune-up as well.

In twelve weeks you will be able to feel and see the impact of walking with God—both physical and spiritual. This is only the beginning, however; this can be the start of an experience that enriches for more than a lifetime. Its impacts can truly be eternal.

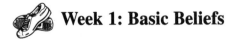 ## Week 1: Basic Beliefs

Our beliefs come to us in varied ways, from childhood Sunday School classes to the witnessing of others. Sometimes we accept some basic elements of our faith without thinking very deeply about them, but the beliefs that are the foundation of our lives deserve our deepest thoughts. This week, reflect on some simple statements that undergird our Christian beliefs. Think about the magnitude of God, about the reality behind your own beliefs, and about how your beliefs have brought you to know, love, and commune with God.

### Monday:

"In the beginning God created the heavens and the earth" (Gen. 1:1).

### Tuesday:

"Therefore, if anyone is in Christ, he is a new creation; the old has gone, the new has come!" (2 Cor. 5:17).

### Wednesday:

"Jesus answered, 'I am the way and the truth and the life. No one comes to the Father except through me. If you really knew me, you would know my Father as well. From now on, you do know him and have seen him' " (John 14:6).

### Thursday:

"If you confess with your mouth, 'Jesus is Lord,' and believe in your heart that God raised him from the dead, you will be saved" (Rom. 10:9).

### Friday:

"Repent, then, and turn to God, so that your sins may be wiped out, that times of refreshing may come from the Lord" (Acts 3:19).

### Saturday:

"I know that my Redeemer lives" (Job 19:25).

### Sunday:

"All men are like grass, and all their glory is like the flowers of the field; the grass withers and the flowers fall, but the word of the Lord stands for ever" (1 Peter 1:23–24).

 **Week 2: Love**

"God is love. Whoever lives in love lives in God, and God in him" (1 John 4:16). This seems to capture the essence of living in communion with God. Love is not something God *does*; He *is* love. If we call ourselves by Christ's name, should we not then put love in the forefront of our lives? The Scriptures say we should, but this is not always easy. There are some very unlovely people in the world, but God did not tell us to love only the well-dressed and well-mannered. This week, consider what Jesus *really* meant when He told us to love one another.

### Monday:

"I am convinced that neither death nor life, neither angels nor demons, neither the present nor the future, nor any powers, neither height nor depth, nor anything else in all creation, will be able to separate us from the love of God that is in Christ Jesus our Lord" (Rom. 8:38–39).

### Tuesday:

"Love one another. As I have loved you, so you must love one another" (John 13:34).

### Wednesday:

"The commandments...are summed up in this one rule: 'Love your neighbor as yourself.' Love does no harm to its neighbor. Therefore love is the fulfillment of the law" (Rom. 13:9–10).

### Thursday:

"[Love] always protects, always trusts, always hopes, always perseveres" (1 Cor. 13:7).

### Friday:

"Give thanks to the Lord, for he is good; his love endures forever" (Psalm 106:1).

### Saturday:

"This is the message you heard from the beginning: We should love one another" (1 John 3:11).

### Sunday:

"And now these three remain: faith, hope and love. But the greatest of these is love" (1 Cor. 13:13).

## Week 3: Forgiveness

Knowing we are forgiven by God is only part of the equation. Forgiveness is also something we are told to give, and this can sometimes be difficult. When others slight us, mistreat us, or hurt us, it is tough to say—and honestly mean—that we forgive. Failure to forgive can be an impediment that separates us from God as well as from others. Is there a person in your life you have found it hard to forgive? Use this week's walks to roll away this impediment.

### Monday:

"If you forgive men when they sin against you, your heavenly Father will also forgive you. But if you do not forgive men their sins, your Father will not forgive your sins" (Matt. 6:14–15).

### Tuesday:

"Bear with each other and forgive whatever grievances you may have against one another. Forgive as the Lord forgave you" (Col. 3:13).

### Wednesday:

"Be kind and compassionate to one another, forgiving each other, just as in Christ God forgave you" (Eph. 4:32).

### Thursday:

"The LORD does not look at the things man looks at. Man looks at the outward appearance, but the LORD looks at the heart" (1 Sam. 16:7).

### Friday:

"The entire law is summed up in a single command: 'Love your neighbor as yourself' " (Gal. 5:14).

### Saturday:

"Do not judge, and you will not be judged. Do not condemn, and you will not be condemned. Forgive, and you will be forgiven" (Luke 6:37).

### Sunday:

"Love your enemies and pray for those who persecute you" (Matt. 5:44).

## 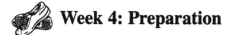 Week 4: Preparation

Christian living does not happen by accident. We come to it through making God central in our lives, by paying attention to what He has told us about what to do, how to think, how to act. There is no checklist to follow, but there are plenty of guidelines. As you walk this week, think about this ongoing process and about how you are preparing yourself for where God might lead you in days to come.

*Monday:*

"Submit yourselves, then, to God. Resist the devil, and he will flee from you. Come near to God and he will come near to you. Wash your hands, you sinners, and purify your hearts, you double-minded" (James 4:7–8).

*Tuesday:*

"Do not conform any longer to the pattern of this world, but be transformed by the renewing of your mind. Then you will be able to test and approve what God's will is—his good, pleasing and perfect will" (Rom. 12:2).

*Wednesday:*

"Create in me a pure heart, O God, and renew a steadfast spirit within me" (Psalm 51:10).

*Thursday:*

"Choose for yourselves this day whom you will serve...As for me and my household, we will serve the LORD" (Josh. 24:15).

*Friday:*

"Your word is a lamp to my feet and a light for my path" (Psalm 119:105).

*Saturday:*

"The righteous cry out, and the LORD hears them; he delivers them from all their troubles" (Psalm 34:17).

*Sunday:*

"Whatever is true, whatever is noble, whatever is right, whatever is pure, whatever is lovely, whatever is admirable—if anything is excellent or praiseworthy—think about such things" (Phil. 4:8).

## Week 5: Christian Living

There are no checklists for Christian living. About two thousand years ago, the Pharisees tried this approach to religion, and Jesus was not amused. Living in Christ is a dynamic process that involves acceptance, obedience, and action. We accept God's reality, we try to be what He wants us to be, and we try to do what He wants us to do. This is an ambitious undertaking! Jesus said, "I have come that they may have life, and have it to the full" (John 10:10). But what must we do to experience

God's abundance in our own lives? As you walk this week, think about what this really requires on a personal level.

### Monday:

"Trust in the LORD with all your heart and lean not on your own understanding; in all your ways acknowledge him, and he will make your paths straight" (Prov. 3:5–6).

### Tuesday:

"Commit your way to the LORD; trust in him and he will do this: He will make your righteousness shine like the dawn, the justice of your cause like the noonday sun" (Psalm 37:5–6).

### Wednesday:

"Love the LORD your God with all your heart and with all your soul and with all your strength" (Deut. 6:5).

### Thursday:

"For God will bring every deed into judgment, including every hidden thing, whether it is good or evil" (Eccl. 12:14).

### Friday:

"I can do everything through him who gives me strength" (Phil. 4:13).

### Saturday:

"And what does the LORD require of you? To act justly and to love mercy and to walk humbly with your God" (Micah 6:8).

### Sunday:

"May the words of my mouth and the meditation of my heart be pleasing in your sight, O LORD" (Psalm 19:14).

 **Week 6: Witnessing**

"Go into all the world and preach the good news to all creation" (Mark 16:15). Jesus' words are pretty clear. This is something we should not need to be told to do. This news is *so* good that we should be shouting it from the housetops. There are people all around us who have not heard or understood the message of our loving

God. Perhaps it is because we have not told them. As you walk this week, think about witnessing and about opportunities *you* might have to share the good news.

### Monday:

"Each one should use whatever gift he has received to serve others, faithfully administering God's grace in its various forms" (1 Peter 4:10).

### Tuesday:

"We are God's workmanship, created in Christ Jesus to do good works, which God prepared in advance for us to do" (Eph. 2:10).

### Wednesday:

"You will be my witnesses...to the ends of the earth" (Acts 1:8).

### Thursday:

"Let your light shine before men, that they may see your good deeds and praise your Father in heaven" (Matt. 5:16).

### Friday:

"But in your hearts set apart Christ as Lord. Always be prepared to give an answer to everyone who asks you to give the reason for the hope that you have" (1 Peter 3:15).

### Saturday:

"Do not forget the things your eyes have seen or let them slip from your heart as long as you live. Teach them to your children and to their children after them" (Deut. 4:9).

### Sunday:

"Love the Lord your God with all your heart and with all your soul and with all your mind.' This is the first and greatest commandment. And the second is like it: 'Love your neighbor as yourself' " (Matt. 22:37–39).

## Week 7: Attitude

What kind of attitude should a Christian project? The sour-faced, overly judgmental stereotype is far from what God has in mind. This holdover from Puritanism is out of step with the joyful, loving, serving example that Christ set for us. Since our attitudes influence others every day, we can only hope that the words of this popular chorus are true: "They will know we are Christians by our love." As you walk this week, think about what it takes to have a Christian attitude, and about how your own attitude might be influencing others.

## Monday:

"Rejoice in the Lord always. I will say it again: Rejoice!" (Phil. 4:4).

## Tuesday:

"Be joyful always; pray continually; give thanks in all circumstances, for this is God's will for you in Christ Jesus" (1 Thess. 5:16–18).

## Wednesday:

"Create in me a pure heart, O God, and renew a steadfast spirit within me" (Psalm 51:10).

## Thursday:

"Delight yourself in the LORD and he will give you the desires of your heart" (Psalm 37:4).

## Friday:

"But be sure to fear the LORD and serve him faithfully with all your heart; consider what great things he has done for you" (1 Sam. 12:24).

## Saturday:

Make sure that nobody pays back wrong for wrong, but always try to be kind to each other and to everyone else" (1 Thess. 5:15).

## Sunday:

"Let your light shine before men, that they may see your good deeds and praise your Father in heaven" (Matt. 5:16).

# 👟 Week 8: Dealing with Anxiety

We may hide them from others and even try to convince ourselves that we do not have them, but everyone has worries and fears. A teenager may worry about being liked by friends, and an adult may worry about how to pay an unexpected bill, but the feelings of uncertainty, fear, and dread are much the same. Fortunately, we do not have to deal with our worries alone. The Bible reminds us time and time again that God will take our burdens from us. All we have to do is lay them at His feet—a good thing to think about while walking this week.

## Monday:

"Cast your cares on the LORD and he will sustain you; he will never let the righteous fall" (Psalm 55:22).

## Tuesday:

"Is anything too hard for the LORD?" (Gen. 18:14).

## Wednesday:

"Be strong and courageous. Do not be afraid…for the LORD your God goes with you; he will never leave you nor forsake you" (Deut. 31:6).

## Thursday:

"The LORD gives strength to his people; the LORD blesses his people with peace" (Psalm 29:11).

## Friday:

"Don't be afraid; just believe" (Mark 5:36).

## Saturday:

"And we know that in all things God works for the good of those who love him, who have been called according to his purpose" (Rom. 8:28).

## Sunday:

" 'For I know the plans I have for you,' declares the LORD, 'plans to prosper you and not to harm you, plans to give you hope and a future' " (Jer. 29:11).

 **Week 9: Faith**

Believing in God is an act of faith. No living person has seen Him or touched Him, yet He is so real and so close that we talk with Him and walk with Him every day. Ours is an era in which we rely on facts, data, and statistics to back up virtually everything; yet we base our entire spiritual life on faith. As you walk this week, think about believing so strongly in what you cannot see and about specific incidents in your own life that have strengthened your certainty of God's presence. Think about your faith, which binds you to God.

## Monday:

"Faith is being sure of what we hope for and certain of what we do not see" (Heb. 11:1).

## Tuesday:

"Those who hope in the LORD will renew their strength. They will soar on wings like eagles; they will run and not grow weary, they will walk and not be faint" (Isa. 40:31).

## Wednesday:

"He who did not spare his own Son, but gave him up for us all—how will he not also...graciously give us all things?" (Rom. 8:32).

## Thursday:

"Everything is possible for him who believes" (Mark 9:23).

## Friday:

"Be strong and courageous. Do not be terrified; do not be discouraged, for the LORD your God will be with you wherever you go" (Josh.1:9).

## Saturday:

Wait for the LORD; be strong and take heart and wait for the LORD" (Psalm 27:14).

## Sunday:

"We fix our eyes not on what is seen, but on what is unseen. For what is seen is temporary, but what is unseen is eternal" (2 Cor. 4:18).

# Week 10: Faith in Action

Salvation is a gift through God's grace, not a reward for what we do. But this does not mean our works are unimportant. "As the body without the spirit is dead, so faith without deeds is dead" (James 2:26). God uses us to do His work here on earth.

Are you putting your faith into action in ways that God finds pleasing? How do you "walk the walk"? Reflect on this question while walking with God this week.

### Monday:

"Let us not love with words or tongue but with actions and in truth" (1 John 3:18).

### Tuesday:

"Religion that God our Father accepts as pure and faultless is this: to look after orphans and widows in their distress and to keep oneself from being polluted by the world" (James 1:27).

### Wednesday:

"Let us not become weary in doing good, for at the proper time we will reap a harvest if we do not give up. Therefore, as we have opportunity, let us do good to all people" (Gal. 6:9–10).

### Thursday:

"Whatever you do, whether in word or deed, do it all in the name of the Lord Jesus, giving thanks to God the Father through him" (Col. 3:17).

### Friday:

"Do not let any unwholesome talk come out of your mouths, but only what is helpful for building others up" (Eph. 4:29).

### Saturday:

"If anyone considers himself religious and yet does not keep a tight rein on his tongue, he deceives himself and his religion is worthless" (James 1:26).

### Sunday:

"Therefore encourage one another and build each other up" (1 Thess. 5:11).

## Week 11: Prayer

It is astounding to realize that God really listens when we pray, but He does. The Scriptures make this crystal clear, as do so many of our own experiences. God does not operate a wish-fulfillment center, so His answers may not always be exactly what and when we have in mind, but He does answer. Best of all, He invites us to make prayer a time of fellowship. This is an incredible blessing! This week accept God's invitation, and make each day's walk a conversation with Him.

## *Monday:*

"Seek the LORD while he may be found; call on him while he is near" (Isa. 55:6).

## *Tuesday:*

"Do not be anxious about anything, but in everything, by prayer and petition, with thanksgiving, present your requests to God. And the peace of God, which transcends all understanding, will guard your hearts and your minds" (Phil. 4:6–7).

## *Wednesday:*

"When you pray, go into your room, close the door and pray your Father, who is unseen. Then your Father, who sees what is done in secret, will reward you" (Matt. 6:6).

## *Thursday:*

"This is the confidence we have in approaching God: that if we ask anything according to his will, he hears us" (1 John 5:14).

## *Friday:*

"The prayer of a righteous man is powerful and effective" (James 5:16).

## *Saturday:*

"Ask and it will be given to you; seek and you will find; knock and the door will be opened to you. For everyone who asks receives; he who seeks finds; and to him who knocks, the door will be opened" (Matt. 7:7–8).

## *Sunday:*

"Pray continually" (1 Thess. 5:17).

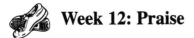 **Week 12: Praise**

As you walk this week, look around you. From the vastness of the sky to the intricacy of a spider's web, you cannot move your eyes without finding evidence of God's greatness. Yet the Bible says that the same God who created all this cares enough about *you* to know even the number of hairs on your head. To have relationship with One so powerful and gentle is astounding and worthy of unceasing praise.

### Monday:

"It is good to praise the LORD…to proclaim your love in the morning and your faithfulness at night" (Psalm 92:1–2).

### Tuesday:

"The heavens declare the glory of God; the skies proclaim the work of his hands" (Psalm 19:1).

### Wednesday:

"Ah, Sovereign LORD, you have made the heavens and the earth by your great power and outstretched arm. Nothing is too hard for you" (Jer. 32:17).

### Thursday:

"You alone are the LORD. You made the heavens, even the highest heavens, and all their starry host, the earth and all that is on it, the seas and all that is in them. You give life to everything, and the multitudes of heaven worship you" (Neh. 9:6).

### Friday:

"Jesus Christ is the same yesterday and today and forever" (Heb. 13:8).

### Saturday:

"God is our refuge and strength, an ever-present help in trouble. Therefore we will not fear, though the earth give way and the mountains fall into the heart of the sea" (Psalm 46:1–2).

### Sunday:

"Give thanks to the LORD for his unfailing love and his wonderful deeds" (Psalm 107:31).

# Samples for Copying

## Walking with God

**Thought for the Walk**

_____

_____

**Prayer Concerns**

_____

_____

_____

_____

_____

**Date/Place** [                  /                    ]

**Distance/Duration** [    .   _miles_ /   _minutes_    _seconds_ ]

**To Do:** (ways to follow up on thoughts from today's walk)

_____

_____

**Special Notes:** (observations or inspirations from the walk)

_____

_____

_____

Months _____ _ _ _ _
Dates _____ _ _ _ _

+2

+1

Starting Weight

-1

-2

-3

-4

-5

-6

-7

-8

-9

-10

-11

W E I G H T

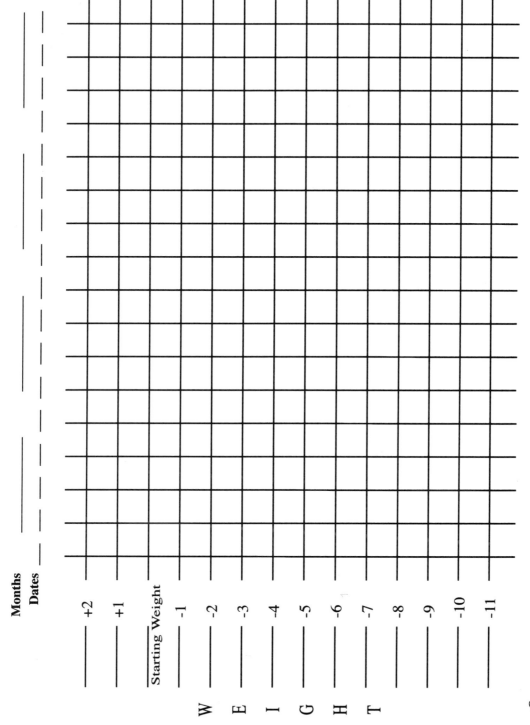

**CHART NO. 2: WEIGHT CHART (FOR WEEKLY WEIGHT LOSS PROGRESS)**

# Heart Rate Chart

Once each week, check your resting heart rate just before taking your fitness walk. Then stop about halfway through that day's walk to check your exercise heart rate.

**Resting Heart Rate**

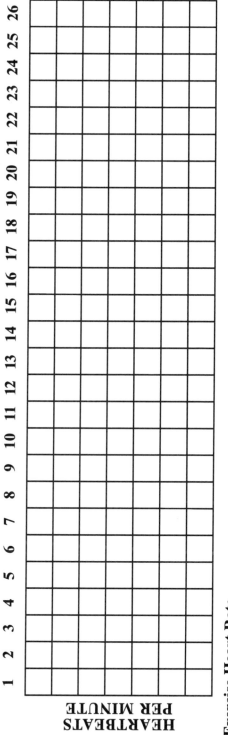

**HEARTBEATS PER MINUTE**

**Exercise Heart Rate**

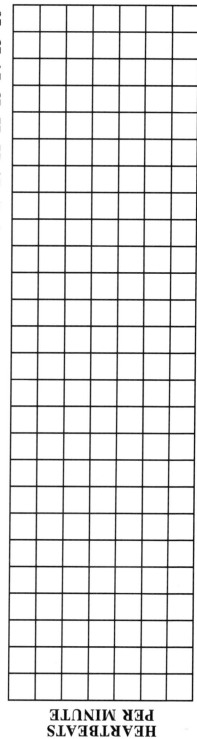

**HEARTBEATS PER MINUTE**

**CHART NO. 5: HEART RATE CHART**